Work in Criminal Justice

An A–Z Guide to Careers

Debbie J. Goodman   Ron Grimming

Upper Saddle River, New Jersey 07458

Library of Congress Cataloging-in-Publication Data

Grimming, Ron.
    Work in criminal justice / Ron Grimming, Debbie J. Goodman.
      p. cm.
    ISBN 0-13-195981-6
     1. Criminal justice, Administration of—Vocational guidance—United States. 2. Law
enforcement—Vocational guidance—United States. I. Goodman, Debbie J. II. Title.

    HV9950.G75 2007
    364.973023—dc22

                 2006046590

Editor-in-chief: Vernon Anthony
Acquisitions Editor: Tim Peyton
Associate Editor: Sarah Holle
Marketing Manager: Adam Kloza
Editorial Assistant: Jillian Allison
Managing Editor: Mary Carnis
Production Liaison: Janice Stangel
Production Editor: Janet Bolton

Manufacturing Manger: Ilene Sanford
Manufacturing Buyer: Cathleen Petersen
Senior Design Coordinator: Mary Seiner
Cover Design: Eva Ruutopold
Printing and Binding: R.R. Donnelley, Harrisonburg
Copy Editor/Proofreader: Maine Proofreading Services

Pearson Prentice Hall™ is a trademark of Pearson Education, Inc.
Pearson® is a registered trademark of Pearson plc
Prentice Hall® is a registered trademark of Pearson Education, Inc.

Pearson Education LTD.
Pearson Education Australia PTY, Limited
Pearson Education Singapore, Pte. Ltd.
Pearson Education North Asia Ltd.
Pearson Education Canada, Ltd.
Pearson Educacion de Mexico, S.A. de C.V.
Pearson Education—Japan
Pearson Education Malaysia, Pte. Ltd.
Pearson Education, Upper Saddle River, New Jersey

10 9 8 7 6 5 4 3 2
ISBN 0-13-195981-6

To Karen, I thank you for your support, your understanding, and your love!

To the men and women who aspire to become members of the criminal justice profession, I encourage you to dream your dream and then make it happen.

—*Ron Grimming*

To Glenn and Connor, my heroes, I love you both more than words can express.

To the past, present, and future criminal justice professionals, I thank you for your exemplary service to our communities.

—*Debbie J. Goodman, M.S.*

CONTENTS

PREFACE

Congratulations! By reading our book, *Work in Criminal Justice,* you have taken an important step toward accomplishing what you ultimately set out to do: work in criminal justice. In order to obtain a long, rewarding, and fulfilling career spanning as many years as you desire, it is important to focus on what it is you want to do and then work hard to achieve your dream.

We encourage you to read the material from start to finish, as each page is important toward helping you figure out "your place" in this exciting industry. The reality is simply that crime in the United States is not going away; therefore, the need for well-educated, well-trained, highly motivated, and extremely competent men and women is at an all-time high!

Employment studies suggest that the average individual will change jobs a minimum of seven times during the course of his or her lifetime! We believe people change jobs so many times because most are simply dissatisfied with the work itself, the salary, or per-haps both. Yet, interestingly, the turnover rates of those employed in the criminal justice profession are much lower when compared with professionals in other industries. Why? We believe one reason is simply that many in the field of criminal justice find their work meaningful, interesting, and financially rewarding. They enjoy what they do and feel they are making a difference.

As you may be aware, according to the U.S. Department of Labor, public safety employment is expected to increase 29 percent by the year 2010. Also, public safety employment is expected to grow faster than the national average for all occupations through 2012. As a result, the future looks bright!

Upon completing our book, *Work in Criminal Justice,* we hope that the search will be narrowed for you and that within these pages you will find critical information about the career of your choice. Once you have found what you have been searching for, we encourage you to pursue your goal with motivation, dedication, and commitment. Don't let anyone or anything stand in your way!

We wish you the best for a fulfilling and gratifying career in criminal justice.

Acknowledgments

We would like to thank Vincent Benincasa, Hesser College, Manchester, NH; Steve Brandl, University of Wisconsin, Richfield, WI; Harold Frossard, Moraine Valley Community College, Pallos Hills, IL; and Michael Grabowski, Santa Rosa Junior College, Santa Rosa, CA for their review of *Work in Criminal Justice*—their input is greatly appreciated.

Ron Grimming

Debbie J. Goodman, M.S.

ABOUT THE AUTHORS

Ron Grimming

Ron Grimming has an extensive and impressive 33-year background in law enforcement. His career in law enforcement began in 1970 as a Special Agent with the Illinois State Police. He served in various investigative assignments, including special task forces targeting criminal activities associated with subversive groups, political and police corruption, illegal drugs, and financial crimes. He was promoted numerous times during his career and attained the rank of Deputy Director of the Illinois State Police, supervising more than 2,500 officers assigned to the investigative and patrol divisions of the department.

In 1993 Grimming was appointed Director of the Florida Highway Patrol, where he managed the activities of 1,740 sworn officers and 528 civilian personnel. Grimming focused the patrol's mission on highway safety through traffic enforcement, accident investigation, prevention of highway violence, interdiction of illegal contraband, investigation of auto theft, and development of public safety education programs. Through Grimming's leadership, the Florida Highway Patrol received the recognition of national accreditation after having its policies and operational procedures scrutinized by a panel of nationally recognized law enforcement experts. Also under Grimming's guidance, the patrol won the prestigious National Chief's Challenge, designating it as having the best traffic safety program in the nation.

During his law enforcement career, Grimming has served as General Chairman of the International Association of Chiefs of Police (IACP), State and Provincial Police Division, which represents the nation's state police and highway patrol organizations on the IACP Board of Directors. Grimming also served as Chairman of the IACP Organized Crime Committee and as President of the State

Law Enforcement Chief's Association. Grimming has an extensive law enforcement training background, having served on Florida's Criminal Justice Standards and Training Commission. He currently serves as Director of Miami Dade College's School of Justice, which has responsibility for college criminal justice degree programs, as well as law enforcement, corrections, and security officer training for Miami-Dade County's criminal justice agencies.

Debbie J. Goodman, M.S.

Debbie J. Goodman, M.S., is the Chairperson of the School of Justice at Miami Dade College. She holds a Master of Science degree in Criminal Justice from Florida International University and a Bachelor of Science degree in Criminology from Florida State University. Ms. Goodman specializes in a wide range of criminal justice topics, including report writing, ethics, communications, human behavior, juvenile justice, criminology, criminal justice, and leadership. She is the author of three national publications: *Report It in Writing, Enforcing Ethics*, and *Florida Crime and Justice.* She is the originator and series editor of Prentice Hall's *PACTS: Police And Corrections Training Series.* Debbie J. Goodman is an adjunct faculty member in the College of Policy Management at Florida International University and was honored in 2002 and 2005 by *Who's Who Among America's Teachers* as one of the nation's most talented college instructors. She is committed to providing quality education and training to police and corrections officers, as well as criminal justice students and practitioners. She resides in South Florida with her husband and son.

CHAPTER ONE

CRIMINAL JUSTICE CAREERS: HOW TO DECIDE

How to Decide on a Career

Here are a few things you can do to enhance your understanding of the career field you anticipate entering:

1. *Read and research.* Review everything you can get your hands on that has to do with the job you think you would like to have (being a probation or parole officer, a cop, a lawyer, etc.). Local libraries, criminal justice textbooks, and the Internet are invaluable resources in this regard!

2. *Get to know people.* Speak with those who are doing the kind of work you are thinking about doing, and meet with them individually for an interview. Prepare your questions prior to the meeting, and learn as much as you can about that job—at least the way each of those people sees it. By talking to more than one such person, you will gain a more accurate impression of the job they do and find out what you need to do to get a job in the industry.

3. *Talk to your professors.* The professors at your local college or university are a good source of information. They can often provide input on job descriptions and job opportunities and can sometimes provide contacts for you in the practitioner community and with graduate schools. They are also a potential source for reference letters as you apply for employment or graduate study.

4. *Participate in an internship program.* Always arrive at your internship site on time, do the best job you can do, ask questions, volunteer for extra assignments, maintain a positive attitude, and be courteous. The image you establish in the eyes of others not only will determine the grade you receive but will have an impact on the assignments you are given and the recommendation of the agency to your future employers. In addition to knowing how to do your job, you should be viewed as someone who is a team player—someone who works well with others and takes directions willingly.

5. *Volunteer.* Do you have any time you can put aside to volunteer for an organization that focuses on your career interest? For example, if you are interested in working with at-risk children, you could volunteer for an organization that offers help to such children or to their families. If you are not sure where to volunteer, contact the kind of agency you would like to work for (probation/parole, police department, department of corrections, etc.) and ask them for a lead. For example, if you want to enter the field of policing, call your local police department and ask if they have connections with any local organizations where you might volunteer. If they have a Toys for Tots program in the winter, maybe you can volunteer to collect toys. Get the idea?

6. *Visit career services offices.* Career services offices can arrange for mock interviews or real interviews (both on and off campus) and can provide an opportunity for you to register in a database so that employers can contact you when relevant job openings become available. Additionally, personnel at career services can provide resources such as tests to help you narrow your career interest based on character traits. Here are a few to consider:

   - The *Self-Directed Search (SDS)* is an easy-to-use tool that allows you to gain insight into your skills and interests and discover career "matches" that fit your personality. Dr. John Holland developed this assessment tool, and he suggests that both people and work environments can be classified according to six basic types: Realistic, Investigative, Artistic,

2

Social, Enterprising, and Conventional (RIASEC). Research has shown that people whose job and work environments most closely match their personal style and interests consider themselves satisfied and successful with the occupational choices they have made.

- The *Myers-Briggs Type Indicator (MBTI)* is used in career counseling to assist you in understanding how your personality preferences can help you decide what you want to do and how to improve your chances of getting what you want. The MBTI was developed by Isabel Myers and Katharine Briggs as a measure of Dr. Carl Jung's theory of psychological types. Results may provide you with information on career options and potential strengths associated with your type, as well as workplace needs.

- *Focus II* is a Web-based computerized career and educational planning system that guides you through a process that enables you to do the following: assess interests, skills, personality, values, and leisure activities; get the facts about occupational options that are aligned with results of assessments; look at educational paths and training programs compatible with your personal attributes; and identify career development needs.

- The *Multiple Intelligence Checklist* evolved from research done by Howard Gardner, Ph.D. The checklist is designed to evaluate the way a person thinks and learns based on life experiences in childhood and the present time. Strengths are identified and associated with nine intelligences. Sample professions are listed under each intelligence area. This tool may help you put your full range of abilities to work.

Work skills are acquired through life and work experiences, as well as education. Every job requires certain skills. Discovering and developing these skills are essential to career success. A variety of career services can provide research, exercises, and activities to help you identify the skills you have and most enjoy using. The skills you have can be the foundation on which you are likely to build your

3

career. You can also learn to evaluate how well your skills match the skills needed in various jobs you find interesting.

Work values are often the determining factors when making career decisions, and they are associated with occupational choices such as achievement, leadership, creativity, security, and adventure, to name a few. You rate the degree of importance each would have in bringing you career satisfaction. Results show clearly the value you place on certain conditions within a workplace setting. This inventory can be quite revealing to you, enabling you to reflect on what conditions are most important in your work.

There are other things you can do to get a better understanding of the kind of job you might like to have, and visiting career-related websites is an excellent place to start! Many offer mock (practice) interview workshops, job-finding services, and much more. We suggest you check your local college or university as well as the Internet for those services provided in your particular geographic area.

How to Find Employment in the Criminal Justice Field

The following list provides you with suggestions on how to find a job in the criminal justice field:

- Seek assistance from placement offices, and attend career seminars.
- Do volunteer work, or participate in an internship program at an agency you would like to work for.
- Read job ads in your local newspaper.
- Call city, county, state, and federal government job information hotlines.
- Search the Internet and agency websites.
- Talk with friends and individuals in the profession for which you seek to work.
- Call local, state, and federal agencies to inquire about job openings, internships, and volunteer opportunities.

- Monitor ads for seeking part-time or full-time work.
- Read trade publications relevant to the job market.
- Go to career centers on college and university campuses.
- Maintain a positive attitude, and never give up your search!
- Let plenty of people know what you are seeking!
- Join criminal justice professional associations.
- Be qualified for the jobs you seek—have the necessary job skills.
- Demonstrate an interest in the criminal justice profession by enrolling and successfully completing criminal justice college course work.

How Are Your Skills?

The exercise below targets skills that are needed in the criminal justice field.

Exercise ▬▬▬▬▬▬▬▬▬▬▬▬▬▬▬▬

After each of the following skills, give an example of how you demonstrate that skill on the lines provided.

Leadership (the ability to guide and direct others to accomplish tasks; to effectively counsel others regarding personal or work-related problems; to motivate others to accomplish tasks and meet goals; to delegate tasks to others effectively; to manage conflict between subordinates; to conduct effective meetings; to establish effective follow-up measures)

_____

_____

_____

_____

_____

_____

Decision making (the ability to perceive the consequences of actions or decisions; to deduce logical courses of action from available data; to establish work priorities; to formulate rational decisions; to evaluate the relative merits of potential courses of action; to generate alternate solutions to problems)

_____

_____

_____

_____

_____

_____

Interpersonal skills (the ability to effectively counsel others regarding personal or work-related problems; to maintain rapport with others; to effectively communicate with others; to deal effectively with irate individuals; to manage conflict between subordinates; to conduct effective meetings)

_____

_____

_____

_____

Decisiveness (the ability to initiate immediate action; to defend one's position when challenged; to maintain an activity or task until completion; to react to the immediate demands presented by a situation)

_____

_____

_____

_____

_____

Perception and analysis (the ability to identify important pieces of information; to identify strengths and weaknesses; to interrelate pieces of information; to identify errors/inaccuracies in written documents)

_____

_____

_____

_____

_____

_____

7

Organization and planning (the ability to establish work schedules; to deliver effective oral presentations; to establish work priorities; to systematically structure tasks; to anticipate future demands that may impact current activities; to establish effective follow-up measures; to effectively maintain several activities simultaneously; to conduct effective meetings)

_____

_____

_____

_____

_____

_____

Adaptability (the ability to adjust approaches to a task according to changing, situational demands; to modify plans based on new information; to generate alternative solutions to problems; to effectively maintain several activities simultaneously; to change activities when interrupted; to react to the immediate demands presented by a situation)

_____

_____

_____

_____

_____

_____

_____

Oral communication (the ability to deliver effective oral presentations; to persuade others when speaking; to conduct effective meetings)

_____

_____

_____

_____

_____

_____

Written communication (the ability to use correct grammar, spelling, structure, punctuation, and vocabulary on written forms and documents)

_____

_____

_____

_____

_____

_____

9

Identify five more strengths you possess that were not identified on the above-mentioned list.

1. _____

   _____

   _____

2. _____

   _____

   _____

3. _____

   _____

   _____

4. _____

   _____

   _____

5. _____

   _____

   _____

What Are Your Personal Characteristics?

By doing the next exercise, you will learn more about yourself and your suitability for a career in criminal justice.

Put a check mark in the boxes that describe you. In the space provided, give an example of how you exhibit each of those characteristics.

❏ **P**—Punctual _____

❏ **R**—Respectful _____

❏ **O**—Organized _____

❏ **F**—Fair _____

❏ **E**—Enthusiastic _____

❏ **S**—Sincere _____

❏ **S**—Self-motivated _____

❏ **I**—Intelligent _____

❏ **O**—Objective _____

❏ **N**—Neat-appearing _____

❏ **A**—Assertive _____

❏ **L**—Logical _____

If you checked at least five boxes, you are well suited for a job in the criminal justice field!

▆▆

Ten Characteristics of Employees in the Criminal Justice Field

Applying certain skills to particular situations is the goal of this exercise.

In the space provided, give an example of how you demonstrate each skill.

1. Has a willingness to help others

_____

_____

_____

_____

_____

_____

2. Exhibits discipline

_____

_____

_____

_____

_____

_____

3. Works well on a team as well as independently

_____

_____

_____

_____

4. Adheres to rules

_____

_____

_____

_____

_____

_____

5. Enjoys working with diverse populations

_____

_____

_____

_____

_____

_____

6. Seeks challenges

_____

_____

_____

_____

_____

_____

7. Possesses problem-solving skills

_____

_____

_____

_____

_____

8. Demonstrates ability to learn new skills

_____

_____

_____

_____

_____

_____

9. Is a good decision maker

_____

_____

_____

_____

_____

_____

10. Respects others

_____

_____

_____

_____

_____

_____

List five additional traits you possess that make you an ideal candidate for a position in the criminal justice profession.

1. _____

2. _____

3. _____

4. _____

5. _____

Note to the Student

An additional recommendation is to interview a professional in the criminal justice field to obtain his or her opinion about the ten characteristics we've identified. Ask the individual which one of these ten characteristics is the most critical to success in the criminal justice field.

"3 T's" of Career Planning

Getting the job you want takes careful thought, a great deal of effort, and commitment to excellence. To get the ball rolling, consider the "3 T's" of planning your career:

1. What **title** do you want to have?
2. What steps will you take **today** to start your career?
3. What **time frame** have you set for yourself to accomplish your career goals?

Respond honestly to each question.

1. This is the **title** I want to have:

_____

_____

_____

_____

_____

_____

2. **Today** I will take these steps to start my career:

_____

_____

_____

_____

_____

_____

3. I will give myself the following **time frame** to accomplish my career goals:

_____

_____

_____

_____

_____

_____

CHAPTER TWO

THE HIRING PROCESS

In order for you to be successful in achieving your goal of becoming a criminal justice professional, you must successfully complete the steps involved in the hiring process.

Before Hiring

1. Job application
2. Entrance exam (civil service examination or basic abilities test)
3. Physical abilities testing
4. Medical examination
5. Interview
6. Psychological testing
7. Background investigation

After Hiring

1. Police Academy training (varies from 10 to 30 weeks)
2. Field training (varies from 30 days to 1 year)

In other chapters of this book, we discuss and provide recommendations on how an applicant can prepare himself or herself for various components of the hiring process.

How to Successfully Dress for the Job Interview

It's probably one of the most overused phrases in job hunting but also one of the most underutilized by job seekers: *dress for success*. When you are selling yourself to a potential employer, the first thing the employer sees when greeting you is your attire. Therefore, you must make every effort to have the proper clothes for the type of job you are seeking. Will dressing properly get you the job? Of course not—but it will give you a competitive edge and a positive first impression.

Should you be judged by what you wear? Perhaps not, but the reality is, you are. Throughout the entire job-seeking process, employers use shortcuts or rules of thumb to save time: With a cover letter, it's the opening paragraph and a quick scan of your qualifications; with a resumé, it's a quick review of your accomplishments; and with a job interview, it's how you're dressed that may set the tone for the interview.

How should you dress? Dressing conservatively is always the safest route, but you should also try to do a little investigating of your prospective employer so that what you wear to the interview makes you look as though you fit in with the organization. If you overdress (a rare but possible situation) or underdress (the more likely scenario), your potential employer may feel that you don't care enough about the job and are ill-suited (no pun intended) for the position.

How do you determine the proper dress for a given job/company/industry? You could call the Human Resources Department where you are interviewing and simply ask. You could also visit the company's office to retrieve an application or other company information and observe the attire of current employees—but make sure you are not there on a "casual day" and thereby misinterpret the dress code.

Finally, do you need to run out and spend a lot of money on clothes for the interview? No, but you should make sure you have at least two sets of professional attire. You'll need more than that down the road, but depending on your current financial condition, two is enough to get started. You can buy more once you have the job or have more financial resources.

Hints for Dressing for Success for Men and Women

Attention to details is crucial, so here are some tips for both men and women. Make sure of the following:

- Well-groomed hair
- Clean and trim fingernails

- Minimal cologne or perfume (or none at all)
- No visible body piercing (beyond conservative ear piercing for women)
- Well-brushed teeth and fresh breath
- No gum, candy, or other objects in your mouth
- Minimal jewelry
- No body odor

Remember: The criminal justice field tends to be traditional and formal, and so should your appearance.

Tips for Men

The standard job-interviewing attire for men is a conservative navy or dark gray two-piece business suit (of natural fibers such as wool, if possible), a white long-sleeved button-down dress shirt, a conservative silk tie (that matches the colors in your suit), and nicely polished dress shoes. If you do not own a suit or if the company is a bit more informal, then you should wear a conservative sports jacket in a dark color (no plaids or patterns) along with nicely pressed dress slacks, a white long-sleeved button-down shirt, a conservative silk tie, and nicely polished dress shoes. Your belt should match your shoes.

If you have a beard or mustache, it should be neatly trimmed. If you have any visible body parts that are pierced, most experts recommend removing all jewelry (including earrings).

Tips for Women

The standard job-interviewing attire for women is a conservative navy or dark gray skirted wool-blend suit. Job experts and employers seem split on the notion of pantsuits, so a skirted suit is a safer choice. Other conservative colors, such as beige or brown, are also acceptable. A blazer with a blouse and skirt is a possible second choice. Skirt length should be slightly below the knee and not shorter than above the knee.

Avoid wearing a dress. Blouses should be cotton or silk and should be white or another light color. Shoes should be low-heeled.

Makeup should be minimal. Lipstick and nail polish should have conservative tones. Pantyhose should be flawless (no runs) and conservative in color. You should opt for a briefcase rather than a purse.

Final Tips

Did you know that more than 90 percent of the decisions about who to bring back for a second interview are made in the first two minutes? This is why how you look is extremely important; after all, there is never a second chance to make a good first impression! Dressing sharply and being well groomed help to make the right first impression. Keep in mind that the interviewer is in charge of selecting people he or she believes will represent the company well.

When you are being interviewed, it is important to dress conservatively. You want your personality, drive, professional commitment, understanding of the business world, etc., to make you stand out, NOT YOUR CLOTHES! Some of the suggestions contained here may not be what you want to hear (e.g., shave your mustache or don't wear colored hose); however, these suggestions are based on research and on the underlying philosophy that it is best to play it safe and conservative when trying to get a job. Looking even slightly unprofessional can cost you the job!

More Things to Think About

Here are two additional considerations:

- *Neatness counts.* Neatness shows that you have pride in yourself and that you care about the interview. Don't wear anything that is uncomfortable because you don't want to be preoccupied with what you're wearing instead of what's going on in the interview. Don't wear anything too complicated; wearing overstated clothing or conspicuous jewelry can give the wrong impression. Visit the restroom before the interview begins to give yourself one last look.

- *Pack an emergency kit.* The emergency kit should include the following: an extra tie/pair of stockings, breath mints, a comb, an extra pair of glasses or contacts, tissues or a handkerchief, and a few safety pins. Don't forget to bring copies of your resumé, transcripts, and three professional reference letters. Your interviewer may request a copy of some of these, and you will look more prepared if you have them readily available. Other good things to bring are a pad of paper, a professional-looking pen, and a date book or organizer.

Again, we are not suggesting you go out and spend a fortune on an Armani or Ralph Lauren suit. We are suggesting that you put your best foot forward and look the part!

How to Polish Your Image

In today's competitive job market, it is essential that job candidates rise above other applicants so that they can be noticed favorably by prospective employers.

Getting the position you want requires the right job skills and the ability to promote yourself in a way that is not offensive. You must look after your own best interests and find a way to bring your assets and past achievements to the attention of employers. Keep in mind there may be hundreds (in some instances, even thousands) of applicants for a limited number of positions; therefore, you need to learn how to toot your own horn.

To let a job interviewer know who you are and what your past accomplishments have been is very important because many employers believe (and rightly so) that an applicant's best indicator of future performance is his or her past performance. The reality is that applicants who learn how to promote and market themselves are much more likely to be successful in landing the job they want.

To assist you in polishing your image, the following tips will be helpful considerations before you go to a job interview:

- Make a list of your skills, interests, and accomplishments that lets the interviewer know who you are, what you have achieved, and how your talents will benefit the agency to which you are applying.

- Don't take undue credit or appear disingenuous.
- Be creative about why you are the right person for the job and how your skills are a good match for the job requirements of the position you are seeking.
- Research the position thoroughly in order to appear knowledgeable about the job and the organization.
- Be enthusiastic and demonstrate genuine interest in the position.
- Know when to brag about yourself and when to be reserved.
- Be a team player.

Exercise

Create a "Best of Me" list of those things that you want to highlight in a job interview. Be sure to include educational accomplishments, athletic achievements, previous employment, job successes, published written works, and any special skills, hobbies, or abilities you possess (languages, licenses, etc.).

_____

_____

_____

_____

_____

_____

_____

_____

_____

_____

_____

How to Find Out about Jobs

Networking

Networking is one of the best ways to find a job. Inform those closest to you (family, friends, acquaintances, classmates, colleagues, and professors) that you are seeking employment. These individuals may be able to help you directly or provide you with a contact who can.

Those skilled at networking maintain ties to individuals in professional associations. As a student, you can maximize your networking potential by joining clubs on campus, volunteering for an agency, and doing community service work.

When networking, always greet every individual you meet professionally. Smile, shake hands, and utilize effective eye contact. Ask individuals for their business cards. If you are a student, have business cards printed with your name, academic major, contact phone number, e-mail address, and future career interest.

It is a competitive field, so get out there and make a good impression!

Exercise

Develop a list of people with whom you would like to network.

_____

_____

_____

Internships

Internships serve several purposes:

1. They provide students with a much-needed opportunity to get a "foot in the door" at an agency in which they seek to be employed.
2. They provide the agency with an opportunity to observe and review the skills, strengths, and weaknesses of interns before deciding whether or not to hire them.
3. They give interns the opportunity to gain valuable hands-on experience in their chosen field.

The internship experience varies from one agency to the next; however, most colleges and universities encourage placement sites to incorporate the following:

- *Agency overview.* The intern spends time in all branches of the agency to get an overall sense of the department's goals, objectives, and mission.
- *Service.* The intern is generally assigned a placement supervisor, and under supervision, the student intern provides services to the agency, as assigned.

Usually, the intern is expected to maintain a weekly log of his or her experiences as a participant observer. The college or university professor will likely require a research paper to be written and submitted before the close of the semester.

The internship experience has many advantages: It allows the intern to achieve firsthand knowledge about an agency, to meet people working in the field, and to make a good impression on future supervisors.

We highly recommend an internship for all men and women who are serious about entering the criminal justice profession.

Exercise

Provide a list of some of the places you would like to do an internship.

_____

_____

_____

_____

_____

_____

Volunteering

Another way to get your foot in the door is to contact the Human Resources Department of a local, state, or federal agency for which you would like to work and offer to volunteer.

Volunteers, like interns, are able to gain valuable insight into an agency's function and provide a service to the agency based on their individual skills and expertise. Volunteers (and interns) who take their role seriously and make significant positive contributions are likely to one day end up on the agency's payroll as employees.

Remember: Hard work pays off!

How to Apply for Jobs

The following sections cover the written documents needed to apply for a job.

Resumé

A *resumé* is a composite of your professional and educational experiences and accomplishments. It must typed, well written, and contain no typographical errors. It should be modified and updated regularly and should contain only accurate information (exaggerations or untruths are never acceptable).

Most students' resumés are divided into the following sections:

- Name, address, phone number, e-mail address (on top of resumé)
- Objective
- Education
- Relevant courses
- Activities/honors
- Work experience

Cover Letter

The cover letter should be addressed to a specific individual or to the supervisor in the Human Resources Department of an agency for which you would like to work.

In the cover letter, you should state clearly the position you seek and provide a synopsis of your relevant experiences, education, and background. Please proofread your work (or have someone else do so). Make certain there are no errors. We believe that mistakes are costly! They give the individual reading your letter a negative impression. If the reader has a negative impression about your written letter, why should he or she be eager to call you, interview you, and offer you a job?

We encourage you to carefully review the following samples of a resumé and a cover letter and to design yours accordingly.

DARREN JOHNSON
1234 Lake Lane
Miami, FL 33120
e-mail: djohnson@mdc.com

Objective: To obtain a position in a law enforcement agency as a sworn police professional.

Education: Miami-Dade College, Miami, Florida Associate in Arts, December 2006
Major: Criminal Justice   Minor: Business
GPA: 3.4

Relevant Courses: Introduction to Criminal Justice,Introduction to Criminology, Criminal Investigations, Juvenile Delinquency, Criminal Law, Human Behavior

Skills: Microsoft Word, PowerPoint, Excel, Publisher

Activities/ Honors: Dean's List, National Honor Society, Criminal Justice Club Member, Tutor

Work Experience: August 2006–December 2006
Tutor, National Honor Society
Involved in assisting college students with academic studies in topics of expertise:

- Criminal Justice, Criminal Law, and Juvenile Delinquency
- Accounting
- Business Administration

January 2006–August 2006
Costco
Involved in serving the organization through providing customer service, stocking shelves, and handling the cash register

January 2005–December 2005
Volunteer, Miami Police Department
Involved in assisting the police department with duties and services, as assigned:

- Going on ride-alongs
- Assisting in Senior Citizen Awareness Day
- Assisting at Miami Art Fair
- Helping to coordinate Gang Prevention Awareness Day

Reference letters available upon request.

December 6, 2006

Ms. Lydia Martinez
Miami Police Department
200 S.W. 1st Place
Miami, Florida 33213

Dear Ms. Martinez:

I am writing to express my interest in the law enforcement position that was advertised in the *Miami Herald* last week.
I am extremely interested in this position as I have just completed my associate's degree at Miami Dade College, earning a cumulative GPA of 3.4.

I have had the opportunity to serve the police department as an intern from January through December 2005. This experience taught me a great deal and solidified my desire to seek full-time employment with your department.

I am very excited about the possibility of receiving training at the Miami Dade College Police Academy and ultimately making a difference in the community. Attached for your review, please find my resumé, which further illustrates my background and experience.

Thank you for your time and consideration, and I look forward to hearing from you.

Respectfully,

Darren Johnson

Reference Letter

A reference letter is a great way for you to shine on paper. Most agencies require a minimum of three professional reference letters to accompany an application packet.

It is our recommendation that you seek reference letters from your professors (in whose classes you performed well!), former supervisors for whom you have worked, and those in the community with whom you have been involved on projects and events.

CHAPTER THREE

INTERVIEW STRATEGIES

Ten Reasons Why the Applicant Doesn't Get the Job

We offer ten reasons why an applicant may not be hired:

1. Lack of education or training
2. Lack of experience
3. Unprofessional appearance
4. Unprofessional demeanor
5. Late arrival for the interview
6. Unrealistic starting salary goals
7. False information on the application and/or resumé
8. Poor evaluation from former supervisor
9. Failure to pass polygraph
10. Unfavorable psychological screening

Exercise

Provide five additional reasons why you think an applicant may not be successful.

1. _____

2. _____

3. _____

4. _____

5. _____

Ten Preparation Questions
for the Job Interview

By doing the following exercise, you will be better prepared for your job interview in the criminal justice field.

Exercise

Write your answers to the following questions; then, have a friend interview you. Practice going over your responses in a mock-interview setting.

1. Tell me about yourself.

   _____

   _____

   _____

   _____

2. Why do you want to work for our agency/department?

   _____

   _____

   _____

   _____

3. Tell me about your work experience.

_____

_____

_____

_____

4. What do you consider to be your three greatest strengths?

_____

_____

_____

_____

5. What do you consider to be your weaknesses?

_____

_____

_____

_____

6. Where do you want to be in five years? Ten years?

_____

_____

_____

_____

7. What are your most significant accomplishments in life?

_____

_____

_____

_____

8. What is your definition of success?

_____

_____

_____

_____

9. How do you think you can benefit our agency/department?

_____

_____

_____

_____

10. Why should we hire you and not another applicant?

_____

_____

_____

_____

Now ask your friend for feedback regarding how you answered these questions. Keep practicing until you feel comfortable and relaxed with your responses.

Ten Do's and Don'ts for the Job Interview

The following list contains what to do—and what not to do—during a job interview:

Do's	Don'ts
1. Do be punctual.	1. Don't be late.
2. Do dress neatly and professionally.	2. Don't wear anything tight, dirty, or revealing.
3. Do speak clearly.	3. Don't mumble.
4. Do be courteous.	4. Don't be rude or disrespectful.
5. Do use good eye contact.	5. Don't avoid eye contact.
6. Do sit up straight.	6. Don't slouch.
7. Do smile.	7. Don't frown or smirk.
8. Do be friendly.	8. Don't be hostile or argumentative.
9. Do be honest.	9. Don't lie.
10. Do thank the interviewer for meeting with you.	10. Don't leave without saying "Thank you" and "Good-bye."

Also, when you shake hands with someone, please have a firm handshake; you want to appear confident and convincing. A weak handshake leaves a negative impression. We highly recommend that you send a thank-you note immediately to the individual with whom you interviewed. This will reinforce your interest in the position and leave a positive impression with the employer.

Ten Questions to Ask Your Future Employer

You may ask any or all of the following if the issues were not addressed during the job interview:

1. When can I expect to hear from you?
2. Does the position require traveling?
3. Does the agency/department provide a training program?
4. What is the starting salary for this position?
5. What are the primary responsibilities of this position?
6. What are the work hours for this position?
7. Who is the supervisor for this position?
8. Does the position call for someone to work independently, on a team, or both?
9. Are there advancement opportunities for someone starting in this position?
10. Does the agency/department offer health insurance and/or a pension plan?

Ten Commonly Asked Questions

Throughout the years, individuals have asked us many questions about deciding on a job that's right for them, getting the job, and keeping the job they want to have in the criminal justice field. Following are ten of the most commonly asked questions and our answers.

1. *Is there a job market in the criminal justice field?*

   Answer: Absolutely—there will always be crime! Because of this, there will be jobs relating to crime prevention, management, analysis, and apprehension. When crime disappears entirely, then jobs may, too. Until that time, there are plenty of jobs for qualified, hardworking, well-educated men and women.

2. *In order to get a job in the criminal justice field, do I need to major in criminal justice?*

    Answer: It depends on what aspect of the field you want to go into. Many police and corrections officers seek majors in criminal justice; other professionals in the field major in law, accounting, psychology, or sociology. Those who go into administrative and management positions major in business, public administration, or public safety. Decide what career you want to pursue, and tailor your major to that role.

3. *Should I pursue a two-year degree or four-year degree in order to get a job in the criminal justice field?*

    Answer: The more education and training you have, the better your chances are of being competitive in this field. Let's face it: When you and another candidate apply for a job and you have a degree and he or she doesn't, who do you think is going to get the job? Most criminal justice agencies/departments regard a degree as your ability to commit and dedicate yourself to a worthy goal. However, a record of all D's and F's is not impressive. In the future, many departments may mandate that representatives of their agencies have a two-year (associate's), four-year (bachelor's) and possibly a graduate (master's) degree. Going to school today may greatly help you in the future!

4. *I know I want to be involved in the field, but how do I figure out what I want to do?*

    Answer: One way to figure it all out is to analyze your strengths and weaknesses as an individual. Ask yourself the following questions:

    - Do I want to take orders from another?
    - Am I willing to work nontraditional hours (midnight, early-morning hours, weekends)?
    - What pay scale am I seeking?
    - Do I want to wear a uniform, a suit, a dress, or relaxed clothing?

37

- Do I want to work independently?
- Do I want to be my own boss?
- Do I want to be an investigator?

Another idea is to talk to as many people as you can who are presently doing what you are interested in doing.

5. *Is it a good idea to participate in an internship program?*

   Answer: Yes! Debbie says this enthusiastically because she's "been there and done that." When she was in her final semester at Florida State University, she participated in an internship program at the Florida State Attorney's Office. She assisted attorneys in preparing for court, sat in on trials, interacted with prominent individuals in the field, and earned college credit. Shortly after she graduated, she applied for (and got!) a full-time (paid) position with the Florida State Attorney's Office. She believes she got the job because she took her role as an intern seriously. As an intern, she was punctual, responsible, and motivated. If you participate in an internship program, do your very best and you just may be offered a job!

6. *What are some of the ups and downs about being a police officer?*

   Answer: Each and every career has its ups and downs. Here are some.

Ups	Downs
Good salary and benefits	Interactions with difficult people
Provision of help to others	High potential for danger
Ability to be promoted	Time away from family (especially during holidays)
Job security	Lack of respect from citizens
Supportive environment	Stress
Interesting work	Boredom

7. *What benefits will I receive working in the criminal justice profession?*

   Answer: It depends on where you work. If you are employed with a state or government agency, you may receive the following:

   - Yearly salary increase (cost of living)
   - Retirement and pension plans
   - Health insurance
   - Vacation time
   - Overtime compensation

8. *How should I answer questions about my background when the answers may provide information that an agency/department may frown upon?*

   Answer: You should answer questions *honestly*. If you are thinking about lying or being deceptive, you may want to consider another profession. The criminal justice profession prides itself on employing honest and ethical men and women who uphold and abide by the laws.

9. *What should I do if I apply for a job in the criminal justice field and don't get it?*

   Answer: How did you learn how to ride a bike or a horse? You practiced! The same is true when it comes to job hunting. If you are faced with rejection, you can let it hold you back or keep trying. Which do you prefer?

10. *How can I make sure I get the job I want?*

   Answer: You can help yourself get the job you want by doing the following:

   - Practicing your interview skills
   - Doing research about the agency/department you hope to work for
   - Getting your college degree
   - Leading a lifestyle that is honorable and ethical

Good luck in achieving your career goals!

CHAPTER FOUR

IMPORTANCE OF ETHICS IN THE CRIMINAL JUSTICE FIELD

As a future criminal justice professional, it is critical that you understand and embrace the importance of ethical conduct and behavior.

The criminal justice profession has been likened to a castle: prestigious, prominent, and deserving of respect. It is critical that the inhabitants of the castle, all current and future criminal justice professionals, commit themselves to upholding and enforcing the law and conducting themselves in accordance with appropriate standards of behavior.

Therefore, in the following pages we provide you with important ethical considerations that are pivotal to your success in the criminal justice field.

The term *ethics*, by definition, is the study of morals—good versus bad, right versus wrong. It's that plain and simple. We're not going to talk about Plato or Aristotle; for our purposes, getting into the history of philosophers, theorists, and ethicists and their views, their perceptions, and their arguments is not necessary at this time.

What *is* necessary is that we in the criminal justice profession (or those who seek to enter it) recognize right from wrong, practice it, believe it, uphold it, and enforce it.

"Yeah, you're right—but . . ." But what? We hear this often from students, colleagues, officers, and trainees.

We believe that in this noble profession of ours, there should be no excuses, no shortcuts, no turning the other cheek. Just do it. Do what is right, moral, just, legal, and appropriate. Those who like to give the "Yeah—but" argument are telling us that they lack the power, control, and discipline on which the foundation of this profession is based.

Every day criminal justice professionals must exercise power, control, and discipline, both on and off duty. How difficult is it to be courteous, pay for your own stuff, tell the truth, and do the best job you are capable of doing while enforcing and upholding the laws of the state in which you live? What's the problem? Let's stick with "Yeah!" instead of "Yeah—but."

Ethics Is a Choice

OK, so now you're coming around a bit. We don't expect you to see it entirely our way, at least not yet. We'll try to further convince you. You realize that as a criminal justice professional, you're in a fishbowl for all to see. People are watching. We love to watch others. Voyeurism? It could be. Whatever you call it, it's reality, so let's be real.

Exercise

If people are watching what you say and do, then how do you want to be perceived?

_____

_____

_____

_____

_____

_____

_____

_____

_____

_____

_____

_____

_____

How you want and choose to be perceived will ultimately determine what you become. Ethics is a choice. It's not a fancy concept; it's a choice. So if you choose to be ethical (from A to Z, soup to nuts, without the "Yeah—buts"), then let's talk.

How to Make an Ethical Decision

Making an ethical decision, whether it is a personal or professional one, is based on Debbie Goodman's ABCD formula:

- *Actions*
- *Beliefs*
- *Conduct*
- *Discipline*

Actions

The way you act, the actions you take day to day, will determine results. Exercise is a good example. Eat well, exercise, don't smoke, don't drink (or if you do, only in moderation), and manage stress, and you should be relatively healthy, according to most doctors. Be intelligent, be hardworking, don't lie, don't cheat, don't steal, and do your best, and you should stay clear of any Internal Affairs (IA) investigations.

Beliefs

Believe in yourself, your department, your profession, your family, your religion, and your friends. Believe in the laws of the land, the policies and procedures of your department, and the good of the cause. Believe that ours is a noble profession, and stand firm on those beliefs. Believe that you can make a positive difference each and every day. Believe that good guys (and gals) prevail and that the bad ones need to be punished.

Conduct

View your own conduct yourself as something everyone is watching: your mom, your dad, your wife, your uncle, your chief, your son or daughter, and God. How do you want them to see you? Let them see you as an honorable, trustworthy, dedicated employee. Let them be proud of you and your actions, not ashamed of and embarrassed by them.

Discipline

If you are tempted, enticed, or intrigued by the possible benefits immediate gratification may bring, you are human. However, if you are weak in character and unable to resist temptations in your job, get out or reconsider even joining this one. We're serious. You need to consider an alternate career because this one is not for you. There are too many good, decent, honest, and loyal criminal justice professionals across the country who put their lives at risk to make communities better and safer places to live.

The Slippery Slope

If you step foot on a slippery slope, do you increase your odds of falling? This is like asking questions such as these: "If you drink alcohol, do you increase your odds of becoming an alcoholic?" "If you gamble, do you increase your odds (no pun intended) of developing out-of-control gambling behavior?" "If you speed, do you increase your odds of getting into an accident?" The answer to all of these questions is a resounding, "Yes!"

The slippery slope theory is one that can be applied to any facet of human behavior. It is important to our discussion of ethics to explore four elements of this theory relative to how we conduct ourselves:

- *Free will*
- *Involved participation*
- *Appropriateness*
- *Consequences*

First, because we live in a free society, we are afforded the opportunity to think and move freely. We would like to present you with a case, a true example of police trainees who found themselves on the slippery slope and slid rapidly downward. After analyzing this scenario, let's look at the four elements of the theory.

Two police trainees, Rick and Dave, were one week shy of graduating from the Police Academy. They had successfully completed all classroom and practical areas of the training curriculum and were preparing to take the state certification exam. On Saturday evening, at approximately 11:30 p.m., they decided to go to an exotic dance club, which featured ladies disrobing onstage. While at the club, they ordered several alcoholic drinks and were becoming increasingly loud and obnoxious. On two occasions, the manager told them to settle down. On the third occasion, the manager told them to leave, at which time Rick stood up, pushed the manager, and stated, "Shut the hell up, Asshole. We're cops!" The manager asked for ID. Dave took out a badge and asked, "OK, Shitface. Satisfied?" The manager went to his office and called the police. Shortly thereafter, the police arrived and arrested Rick for battery, intoxication, and impersonation of an officer: Dave was arrested for intoxication and impersonation of an officer. Their careers in law enforcement were over. Now, using this scenario, let's address the four elements of the slippery slope theory.

Free Will

As you consider the issue of free will (the ability to make a voluntary choice), do you think Rick and Dave exercised free will? The answer is yes.

Which statements are true?

1. Rick and Dave decided to go to the exotic dance club.
2. Rick and Dave drank several alcoholic beverages.
3. Rick and Dave decided to get loud and obnoxious.
4. Rick pushed the manager.
5. Rick stated that they were cops.
6. Dave showed the manager a badge.
7. Rick and Dave were disrespectful to the manager.

As you review these statements, you will agree that all are true based on the facts of the case. Let's address the second element of the slippery slope theory.

Involved Participation

The slippery slope theory maintains that behaviors may quickly become increasingly worse, depending on the extent to which the participants are involved. In the Rick and Dave case, it appears as though both parties were involved in the following:

- Drinking alcoholic beverages
- Becoming loud and obnoxious
- Using profanity
- Impersonating an officer

What do you think would have happened if the two trainees had decided to go to the movies or to a football game instead? Chances are pretty good that they would have graduated from the Police Academy, passed the state certification exam, and started their career in the profession.

Appropriateness

On a daily basis, each of us must examine the appropriateness of our behavior. An easy way to make this determination is to consider the following three areas:

1. *Status.* One's status (e.g., position, rank, title, and professional affiliation) should be considered when deciding on places to go, people to associate with, and behavior to participate in.
2. *Time.* Is the time of day a factor for consideration regarding appropriateness? Yes. Different things may happen at 11:30 a.m. versus 11:30 p.m. Right?
3. *Place.* Is the place one is planning to go (e.g., a bar, a church, the beach, a casino) an appropriate place given one's status? That's for you to decide.

Consequences

The fourth element of the slippery slope theory involves consequences. Remember the saying, "Let your conscience be your guide." When analyzing ethics, if the consequences of potential actions appear stringent and potentially damaging to your health, safety, and career, let your conscience be your guide: Refrain. By not stepping onto the slippery slope and taking the high road instead, you are using your most impressive weapon: your brain.

An Ethics Discussion

"Is it OK for an officer to accept free coffee, food, and other stuff?" asked the inquisitive trainee. The answer to this question has been debated for years and will continue to be for years to come.

In order to provide an appropriate response to this often-asked question, we need to analyze the definition of the term "ethics." Ethics means principles of accepted rules of conduct for a particular individual or group as mandated by law, policy, or procedure. Let's examine each component of this definition of ethics.

Principles of Accepted Rules of Conduct

Almost everything in life is based on rules. Sports enthusiasts are familiar with the rules of football. When a player is cited for an illegal face mask, he has broken an important rule of the game and will incur a penalty. That penalty will adversely impact him as well as his team-mates. At the Police Academy, a trainee who violates an institutional rule may find himself or herself facing counseling, a reprimand, or stringent disciplinary action. In a police or corrections department, an officer who does not adhere to the rules may encounter unwanted media attention, liability, and possibly termination. Therefore, it's fair to say that a significant consequence may act as a deterrent for future inappropriate behavior; however, if no consequence exists or if the consequence is not enforced, the rule breaker may be inspired to continue along a path of inappropriate conduct.

For a Particular Individual or Group

Doctors, lawyers, accountants, and police officers have something in common: These professionals have strict guidelines they must adhere to in order to maintain their certification. Professionals of this caliber are held to high standards, and each group member has a unique ethical code to which he or she must comply. Failure to comply may result in decertification.

As Mandated by Law, Policy, or Procedure

When something is in writing, we notice it, read it, refer to it, remember it, and ultimately *adhere* to it. Therefore, if criminal justice directors, administrators, trainers, practitioners, and educators are serious about enforcing ethics, they must work collaboratively to implement specific state (and even federal) guidelines that police and corrections departments must follow. Additionally, department representatives could reinforce these guidelines by writing policies and procedures that explain, clearly and completely, the behaviors that will and will not be tolerated for officers representing their police or corrections department. The following illustration easily could be added to a department's standard operating procedures under the ethics category.

The following behaviors are unacceptable and are viewed by this department as unethical:

1. Accepting gratuities (e.g., gifts, favors, money, or anything given to you for free)
2. Using unnecessary force (e.g., physical abuse, emotional mistreatment, or roughing up suspects in custody)
3. Practicing discrimination (mistreating individuals on the basis of race, age, gender, religion, culture, sexual preference, or national origin)
4. Lying in any form (e.g., creating facts to incriminate or protect another)
5. Violating laws, rights, or procedures (e.g., intentionally making a false arrest, filing a false report, or purposely ignoring departmental procedures)

Many criminal justice agencies are asking future employees to respond to ethics-related questions and scenarios as part of the interview process. Review the following ethics scenarios from Debbie Goodman's *Enforcing Ethics* workbook available through Prentice Hall (www.prenhall.com or 800-526-0485). Think critically and carefully about your answers. Good luck!

THE CLUB SANDWICH

This is your first week on the job as a newly sworn police officer. You performed well in all of your classes at the Police Academy. You particularly enjoyed the ethics class. You found the scenarios interesting, and you made a promise to yourself that you would never accept freebies or act in a manner unbecoming to the profession. On this day, you and two senior officers clear a lunch break with the dispatcher. You enjoy a pleasant lunch: a club sandwich. After the meal, your fellow officers get up to leave as you reach for your wallet. One officer asks, "What are you doing?" You respond, "I'm paying for my lunch." He says, "Kid, it's on the house. That's why we eat here." You respond, "At the Police Academy, we were taught that accepting discounted or free meals is unethical." Both officers laugh and say, "Kid, forget the Police Academy. This is the real world."

Ethically, what should you do?

_____

_____

_____

_____

_____

_____

_____

_____

Scenario 2

THE PERJURER

You and your partner are dispatched to a robbery call. The dispatcher describes the suspect as a white male juvenile, approximately 15 to 17 years of age, wearing a black T-shirt, blue jeans, and tennis shoes. A few blocks east of the scene, your partner sees someone who fits the suspect's description. Your partner exits the patrol car and shouts, "Police! Stop!" The juvenile starts running, and your partner runs after him. Moments later your partner fires his revolver, shooting the juvenile in the back. You call fire and rescue; they respond and transport the juvenile to the hospital. Meanwhile, your partner takes you aside and says, "I need you to back me. You gotta help me. No matter who asks, tell them it looked like the kid was about to draw a weapon." (The truth is, the juvenile did not have a weapon.) Later that day, Officer Thomas from Internal Affairs asks you to tell him what happened.

Ethically, what should you do?

_____

_____

_____

_____

_____

_____

_____

_____

THE FAVOR

You are a corrections officer who works in a maximum-security facility. Yesterday, you misplaced your keys. Fortunately, Inmate Jones found your keys, and he returned them to you. Tonight, he tells you he received a letter from his wife, who is filing for divorce. He asks you if he can use the phone to call her. He already used the phone earlier today, and it is now "lights out."

Ethically, what should you do?

_____

_____

_____

_____

_____

_____

_____

_____

_____

_____

_____

_____

THE WALLET

You are an off-duty officer who has just completed a three-mile run. You decide to cool off and rest under a big oak tree. You sit down under the tree and see a brown leather wallet close by. Curiosity gets the best of you, and you open the wallet. Interestingly enough, you find credit cards, identification, and $300 in cash. Nobody else is around.

Ethically, what should you do? If you found $3,000, $30,000, or more, what should you do?

_____

_____

_____

_____

_____

_____

_____

_____

_____

_____

_____

_____

_____

THE HARASSER

You are a probationary police officer; in two weeks, you will be on permanent status with your department. Your immediate supervisor, Sergeant Richards, repeatedly makes inappropriate comments to your colleague, a female probationary police officer, regarding her "beautiful face" and "knockout figure." This morning, you overhear Sergeant Richards tell her, "If you don't go out with me, you'll never make it past your probationary stage." She decides to file a report.

Ethically, what should you do?

_____

_____

_____

_____

_____

_____

_____

_____

_____

_____

_____

_____

CHAPTER FIVE

ARE YOU FIT FOR DUTY?

We believe that physical fitness is vital to criminal justice professionals for many reasons. Accordingly, individuals seeking a criminal justice career should begin to prepare themselves for a rigorous physical and mental training program before they enter the Police Academy.

Importance of Physical Fitness

In fact, most criminal justice agencies and training academies require prospective recruits to undergo a complete physical examination by a doctor prior to academy training commencing. This requirement exists to ensure that new recruits are physically capable of handling the demands of an intensive training program, which may consist of doing calisthenics, running, weight lifting, practicing defensive tactics, using firearms, and doing various other tactical scenarios requiring physical stamina.

Once admitted into the Police Academy, you will be required to participate in a vigorous physical fitness program, with your progress being measured throughout the training program. You will be expected to achieve significant gains in your physical fitness capability and (where appropriate) achieve any necessary weight loss or gain. Individual assessments are often conducted so that performance and progress can be tracked. This is accomplished through administering physical fitness tests at the beginning of academy training and again at the conclusion of training. Results are measured by progress attained by each recruit.

After completing Police Academy training, criminal justice recruits must remain physically capable of performing their duties and handling the stress associated with the emotional pressure of their profession. Criminal justice as a profession holds the distinction (unfortunately) of having the highest rates of heart disease, diabetes, and suicide of any profession. This unfortunate statistic signals the importance of maintaining a lifelong fitness lifestyle so that officers can better cope with the potential for stress-related diseases.

Officers who remain physically fit throughout their careers are better able to handle the day-to-day stress of the job and are better prepared to handle the emergency incidents they frequently encounter. In other words, during a physical confrontation with someone, the officer must be able to control a suspect or physically restrain an arrestee, making physical fitness an essential part of officer survival.

Physical fitness is considered an important component of an individual's overall health condition, and as such, it is directly related to an officer's physiological readiness to perform at maximum physical readiness when required.

When considering physical fitness, experts agree that there are three main categories:

1. *Aerobic capacity.* This refers to the cardiovascular endurance of the heart and the vascular system's capacity to transport oxygen. It should be noted that low aerobic capacity can be a risk factor for heart disease.
2. *Strength.* This pertains to the ability of muscles to generate force. Upper body strength and abdominal strength are important areas because low strength levels have a bearing on upper torso and back disorders. Additionally, low upper body strength may be detrimental to an officer who needs to defend himself or herself during a physical confrontation.
3. *Flexibility.* This references the range of motion of the joints and muscles. Lack of lower back flexibility is a major risk factor for lower back ailments.

Physical fitness has been determined to be a bona fide occupational qualification (BFOQ), and as such job analysis has demonstrated that these three fitness areas are predictive of job performance ratings, use of sick time, and recognition received by officers for excellent performance. Studies have also indicated a positive relationship between physical conditioning and performance during Police Academy training.

These three factors should provide strong evidence of the overall importance of physical fitness to the individual contemplating a career in the criminal justice profession.

How to Prepare for a Physical Agility Test

To assist you in preparing for the Police Academy and in developing a physical fitness lifestyle, the following exercises will be beneficial because they focus on the most common physical agility tests given by criminal justice agencies.

In preparing for a criminal justice physical agility test, it's essential to recognize that most fitness tests consist of variations of the sit-and-reach test (flexibility), sit-up test (abdominal strength), and push-up test (upper body strength) as well as a run of one and a half miles (aerobic capacity). Various agencies may modify or even eliminate one or more of these categories, but generally speaking, if a candidate prepares for these fitness tests, he or she will be prepared for any variation offered by an agency.

Candidates are encouraged to prepare for the test by actually performing progressive exercises that correspond with the events on the physical fitness test. *Of course, a medical examination is recommended before beginning any physical training program.*

The following is a recommended training program to assist you in achieving the required fitness level to successfully pass the pre-employment fitness test.

1. *Preparation for the sit-and-reach test.* Performing sitting types of stretching exercises daily will increase your performance in this area. There are two recommended exercises:
   - *Sit and reach.* Do five repetitions of the exercise. Sit on the ground with legs straight out in front of you. Slowly extend forward at the waist and extend the fingertips toward the

toes (keeping legs straight and against the floor). Hold for ten seconds.

- *Towel stretch.* Sit on the ground with the legs straight out in front of you. Wrap a towel around the feet, holding each end of the towel with each hand. Lean forward and pull gently on the towel while extending the torso toward the toes.

2. *Preparation for the sit-up test.* The progressive routine is to do as many bent-leg sit-ups (hands behind the head) as possible in one minute. At least three times a week, do three sets (three groups of the same number of repetitions as you did in one minute).

3. *Preparation for the push-up test.* If you have access to weights, determine the maximum weight you can bench-press at one time. Take 60 percent of that poundage as your training weight. You should be able to do eight to ten repetitions of that weight. Do three sets of eight to ten repetitions, adding two and a half pounds every week.

4. *Preparation for the 1.5-mile run.* Below is a graduated schedule that would enable you to perform at maximum effort for the 1.5-mile run. If you can advance the schedule on a weekly basis, then proceed to the next level. If you can do the distance in less time, you should be encouraged to do it.

WEEK	ACTIVITY	DISTANCE	TIME (MINUTES)	FREQUENCY
1	Walk	1 Mile	17–20	5/Week
2	Walk	1.5 Miles	25–29	5/Week
3	Walk	2 Miles	32–35	5/Week
4	Walk	2 Miles	28–30	5/Week
5	Walk/Jog	2 Miles	27	5/Week
6	Walk/Jog	2 Miles	26	5/Week
7	Walk/Jog	2 Miles	25	5/Week

(continued)

WEEK	ACTIVITY	DISTANCE	TIME (MINUTES)	FREQUENCY
8	Walk/Jog	2 Miles	24	5/Week
9	Jog	2 Miles	24	5/Week
10	Jog	2 Miles	22	5/week
11	Jog	2 Miles	21	5/week
12	Jog	2 Miles	20	5/week

Students who already are in good physical condition will be able to quickly achieve the necessary results to pass the physical fitness test; however, students who need to improve their conditioning should plan to prepare for the exam at least 12 weeks before the scheduled exam date. This will provide ample time to reach the desired fitness level and will assist in preventing injuries during training.

It is recommended that candidates contact the respective criminal justice agency to which they intend to apply and obtain the specific thresholds for passing scores for each fitness dimension. Candidates will then be able to monitor their training progress and know when they have achieved the appropriate fitness level to pass each required exercise.

Remember: The importance of physical fitness for criminal justice professionals cannot be overemphasized. The job of a criminal justice practitioner depends heavily on his or her ability to utilize strength and endurance when required.

Diet for Fitness

Exercise alone is not enough to sustain a healthy, fit lifestyle. It must be coupled with a healthy diet. Eating right is vital to promoting health and reducing the risk of disability or death due to chronic diseases such as heart disease, cancer, diabetes, stroke, and osteoporosis.

According to government projections, only one-fourth of U.S. adults eat the recommended servings of fruits and vegetables each day, and these poor eating habits are usually established during childhood. More that 60 percent of young people eat too much fat, and less than 20 percent eat the recommended servings of fruits and vegetables. These latter statistics are particularly alarming as our future criminal justice candidates will come from this generation.

Although we will not recommend a specific type of diet for our future criminal justice professionals, we will provide general guidelines and encourage you to consult the Dietary Guidelines for Americans, which can be found on the U.S. Department of Agriculture's website.

What Is a Healthy Diet?

The Dietary Guidelines for Americans describes a healthy diet as one that does the following:

- Emphasizes fruits, vegetables, whole grains, and low-fat or fat-free milk and milk products
- Includes lean meats, poultry, fish, beans, eggs, and nuts
- Is low in saturated fats, trans fats, cholesterol, salt (sodium), and sugars

If followed, these general guidelines not only will produce a nutritional and healthy eating plan but will provide sufficient fuel for the body's optimal physical well-being and performance. Additional benefits include both weight loss, which will reduce the strain on your heart and assist in controlling blood sugar, and lowered cholesterol, which will help lower the risk of heart disease and stroke.

Perhaps one of the most common problems faced by criminal justice candidates as they prepare for Police Academy training and as they progress through their careers is maintaining the proper weight. There is a very simple rule that, if put into practice, will certainly make weight control a thing of the past: Balance the number of calories you eat with the number you use each day. Although this rule sounds very basic, it makes perfect sense when you think about it. If the body takes in more fuel than it uses, that results in weight gain; if it takes in less fuel than it uses, that results in weight loss. To determine your calorie balance, multiply your weight in pounds by 15 (e.g., 15×160 lbs. = 2,400 calories). Individual metabolism and exercise will impact each individual's calorie balance, but this formula provides a general guideline for calorie consumption.

It's important to remember that your food and physical activity choices each day affect your health—how you feel today, tomorrow, and in the future.

If you establish a well-conditioned fitness and dieting lifestyle early in life, you should be able to cope better with stress, avoid injury and disease, and enjoy a healthy lifelong career in criminal justice.

CHAPTER SIX

YOUR A–Z GUIDE TO LOCAL, STATE, AND FEDERAL CRIMINAL JUSTICE CAREERS

For your convenience, we have provided a listing and explanation of potential criminal justice careers, including local, state, and federal positions, which are utilized and widely available in various jurisdictions throughout the United States.

As you narrow your search and begin to apply for specific positions, we encourage you to thoroughly research the agencies to which you submit applications. The research you conduct not only will assist you in making an informed career choice but also will benefit you in demonstrating specific job-related knowledge during interviews with prospective employers.

Additional information sources on specific positions are widely available on agency websites, in criminal justice publications, at job fairs, in agency brochures, and through newspaper advertisements.

When choosing a particular career option from those listed on the pages that follow, keep in mind that each level of government (local, county, state, and federal) has its own benefits and salaries and that the various job titles have different pay grades. Although it is not necessarily true in all regions of this country, generally state and federal criminal justice positions have the greatest prestige and highest pay; however, applicants to state and federal positions should recognize that they will likely have to relocate.

Below are entry-level minimums to give you an idea of starting salaries for various positions. Note that many regions of the country have higher entry-level salaries:

- Municipal (city) jobs—about $30,000
- County jobs—about $25,000

- State jobs—about $32,000
- Federal jobs—about $40,000

Corrections officers' pay varies significantly from state to state, with the larger states (and bigger prison systems) having an entry-level salary in excess of $30,000 a year.

In law enforcement agencies, usually larger departments having many different job titles offer greater opportunities and higher entry-level salaries, with many starting new officers at pay in excess of $40,000 per year.

We encourage you to check with specific agencies as you narrow your job search because criminal justice salaries change frequently, based on collective bargaining agreements and government-initiated salary adjustments.

Careers in Law Enforcement

The following list presents many of the jobs available in law enforcement.

AIR SAFETY INVESTIGATOR

Investigation of aircraft incidents

Preparation of factual reports of findings

Required pilot-in-command (flight time) hours

Knowledge of aircraft design and aviation practices

ALCOHOL, TOBACCO, AND FIREARMS INSPECTOR

Provision of industrial regulations and collection of taxes from alcohol and tobacco industries

Provision of information to alcohol and ATF agents

Use of firearms not required

ALCOHOL, TOBACCO, AND FIREARMS SPECIAL AGENT

Investigation of federal laws regarding firearms or explosives

Enforcement of laws for liquor and tobacco industries

Assistance for Secret Service in presidential protection when needed

Use of firearms required

CUSTOMS AIDE

Assistance with responsibilities of other Customs Service positions

Excellent entry-level position with possibility of advancement to higher titles

Two years of experience required

CUSTOMS CANINE ENFORCEMENT OFFICER

Training and use of dogs to enforce rules and regulations pertaining to smuggling of controlled substances

Possible advancement to other Customs titles

No written test, but three years of relevant experience required

CUSTOMS IMPORT SPECIALIST

Determination of value of incoming merchandise and classification of these goods under tariff

Use of schedules to determine correct duty and taxes required

Possible assignment to seaport, airport, or land-order post

CUSTOMS INSPECTOR

Enforcement of compliance with tariff laws and prevention of smuggling, fraud, and cargo theft

Detection of illegal importation and exportation of narcotics and other contraband

Search of holds of ships

CUSTOMS PATROL OFFICER

Member of tactical land, sea, and air effort aimed at prevention of smuggling

Possible patrol by foot, car, boat, or aircraft

Potentially hazardous work

Duty station (when possible) of applicant's choice

CUSTOMS PILOT

High technical requirements of career in law enforcement

Duties involving air surveillance of illegal duties

Apprehension, arrest, and search of violators

CUSTOMS SPECIAL AGENT

Investigation of criminal fraud by use of revenue, countervaluing, and theft of major cargo

Investigation of illegal importation and exportation of contraband

Use of firearms required

DEPARTMENT OF LABOR, LABOR AND PENSION COMPLIANCE INVESTIGATOR

Investigation (as team member) of compliance with labor laws

Examination of union and organization documents and contracts to ensure compliance

Knowledge of investigatory techniques

DEPUTY SHERIFF

Uniformed law enforcement position

Position similar to that of police officer and trooper but with court and corrections responsibilities

Use of firearms required

DEPUTY U.S. MARSHAL

Provision of federal court security, protection of federal witnesses, investigation of federal fugitives, prisoner transport, and custody of federal prisoners

Three years of relevant experience or college degree, as well as passing grade on marshal's exam

Worldwide travel

DIPLOMATIC SECURITY SPECIAL AGENT

Provision of security for foreign service personnel

Provision of protection for U.S. Secretary of State and other foreign dignitaries

Arrest authority

DISPATCHER

Reception and dispatch of emergency and routine calls to patrol units

Performance of record checks

Maintenance of computerized and written reports

Operation of sophisticated computer equipment

DRUG ENFORCEMENT SPECIAL AGENT

Authority to stop flow of illegal drugs

Possible geographic relocation at appointment

Long hours

Undercover work

College degree required

Use of firearms required

ENVIRONMENTAL CONSERVATION OFFICER

Outdoor work required

Possible long and irregular hours

Ability to work independently

FEDERAL AIR MARSHAL

Response to criminal incidents on aircraft

Authority to carry firearms and make arrests

Preservation of safety of crew and passengers on commercial aircraft

Top secret clearance required

Maximum age limit of 40

FEDERAL BUREAU OF INVESTIGATION, SPECIAL AGENT

Member of nation's most prominent law enforcement agency

Authority over kidnapping, bank robbery, organized crime, civil right violations, fraud, espionage, and terrorism (among others)

College degree and relevant experience required

Use of firearms required

FEDERAL PROTECTIVE SERVICE OFFICER/CRIMINAL INVESTIGATOR

Wide law enforcement powers over properties

Bachelor's degree and exam required

Use of firearms required

FISH AND WILDLIFE SERVICE, SPECIAL AGENT

Investigation of violations of federal fish and wildlife laws

Protection, maintenance, control, and improvement of national fish and wildlife resources

Hiring based on education and experience

IMMIGRATION AND NATURALIZATION SERVICE, BORDER PATROL AGENT

Detection and prevention of illegal entry of persons into United States

Work locations along 8,000 miles of land and water defining U.S. territory

Ability to read Spanish and to speak it fluently

IMMIGRATION AND NATURALIZATION SERVICE, CRIMINAL INVESTIGATOR

Investigation of violations of criminal and statutory provisions of immigration and naturalization laws

Some undercover assignments

Possible relocation

IMMIGRATION AND NATURALIZATION SERVICE, DEPORTATION OFFICER

Control and removal of persons who have been ordered deported or have been required to leave the United States

Travel required

Use of firearms required

IMMIGRATION AND NATURALIZATION SERVICE, INSPECTOR

Work locations at land ports of entry, airports, seaports, and places where people enter United States from other countries

Authority to prevent entry to United States of persons who are illegal and to permit entry of those who are admissible

Uniform required

INSPECTOR GENERAL

Internal investigations of waste, fraud, and mismanagement in federal agencies

College degree required

Excellent written and communication skills

INTELLIGENCE SUPPORT ANALYST

Collation of statistical data for law enforcement agencies

Preparation and analysis of reports and use of automatic/computer information systems

Strong academic grades (high GPA)

INTERNAL REVENUE SERVICE, CRIMINAL INVESTIGATOR

Investigation of charges of criminal and civil violations of Internal Revenue laws

Excellent written and communication skills

Potential for irregular hours

INTERNAL REVENUE SERVICE, INTERNAL SECURITY INSPECTOR

Investigations to ensure honesty and integrity maintained at all levels of service

Possible stressful job conditions

Travel possible

INVESTIGATOR (MUNICIPAL, COUNTY, STATE)

Provision of criminal or civil investigative support to agencies with specific responsibilities

College degree and some related experience generally required

Possible requirement to carry firearms

NATIONAL PARKS POLICE

Provision of law enforcement services in national parks

Possible relocation

Training in use of firearms

NAVAL INVESTIGATIVE SERVICE/CRIMINAL INVESTIGATOR

Performance of criminal investigations

Possible tour of duty

Baccalaureate degree required

POLICE OFFICER (MUNICIPAL)

Uniform required

Protection of lives and property of public

Preservation of law and order

Excellent communication skills

Use of firearms required

POSTAL INSPECTOR

Criminal and audit investigations of U.S. Postal Service

Security and administrative duties

Frequent travel

SECRET SERVICE AGENT

Executive protection and investigation of crimes against U.S. currency

Frequent travel

Stringent physical requirements

College degree required

Use of firearms required

SECRET SERVICE UNIFORMED OFFICER

Provision of security through a network of vehicular and foot patrols, fixed posts, and canine teams at White House buildings in which presidential offices are located and at main Treasury Building and Treasury Annex in Washington, D.C.

Job site exclusively in Washington, D.C.

Use of firearms required

SECURITIES COMPLIANCE EXAMINER

Top 10 percent of college graduating class or 3.45 overall GPA

Keen analytical skills and ability to plan and organize

Bachelor's degree required (any major)

STATE POLICE OFFICER/STATE TROOPER

Public safety responsibilities and patrol activities on state and interstate highways

Enforcement of motor vehicle and criminal laws

Traffic enforcement

Statewide criminal investigation authority

Use of firearms required

Exercise

Of the above-listed careers, which position most interests you?

_____

_____

_____

_____

_____

_____

_____

_____

Careers in the Courts

In this section, we offer various occupations associated with the court system.

ATTORNEY/LAWYER

Interpretation of laws, ability to act as advocate/advisor, and presentation of cases in court

Research for and writing of legal briefs

Representation of clients in civil or criminal courts

BAILIFF

Uniformed law enforcement officer entrusted to provide courtroom security

Escort for prisoners and jury members

High school diploma and passing grade on civil service examination required

CHILD AND YOUTH COUNSELOR

Assistance to children and families in overcoming trauma of crime

Assistance to court in assessing child's cognitive ability and emotional state before start of case

Knowledge of courts and criminal justice system helpful

COURT ADMINISTRATOR

Performance of administrative and management functions within court system

Assistance for judge with court calendar, case flow, and personnel management

Knowledge of law important

COURT CLERK

Clerical assistance for variety of administrative responsibilities

Maintenance of case records

Preparation of statistical reports

COURT LIAISON COUNSELOR

Assistance and counsel for defendants charged with crimes

Evaluation and initiation of treatment plans

Referrals to support agencies

COURT REPORTER (SHORTHAND REPORTER)

Recording of all trial proceedings with use of stenographic machine

Passing grade on certifying exam as court reporter

Knowledge of legal vocabulary essential

COURT REPRESENTATIVE

Ascertainment of eligibility for alternative services instead of
detention

Significant interactions with defendant population

Related experience and education required

CRISIS COUNSELOR

Provision of services to victims of domestic violence, incest, or
rape and to runaway youth

Provision of services such as crisis intervention, short-term
counseling, and concrete services

Bachelor's degree plus two years of relevant experience required

DOMESTIC VIOLENCE COUNSELOR

Assistance and counsel for victims of domestic violence

Strong human relations skills

Varied work hours

JUDGE

Oversight of legal process in courts of law

Safeguarding of rights, determination of legal positions, and instructions to jury

Determination of sentences, bail, and damages

PARALEGAL/LEGAL ASSISTANT

Performance of clerical and administrative duties for lawyers

Research for and preparation of cases

Procurement and drafting of legal documents

PRETRIAL SERVICES OFFICERS (U.S. DISTRICT COURTS)

Investigation and supervision specialist

Advice to courts on pretrial release, detention, and release conditions

Duties similar to those of probation officer

RELEASE ON OWN RECOGNIZANCE (ROR) INTERVIEWER

Interview of and background information on defendants

Formulation of release recommendations to judges

Frequent court appearances

RESEARCH ANALYST/STATISTICIAN

Preparation and evaluation of statistical reports

Strong math and computer skills

Bachelor's degree required, but master's degree preferred

RUNAWAY COUNSELOR

Assistance to runaway children by discussing dangers of living on street

Experience in area of counseling, peer counseling, or human services preferred

Work via a hotline number given out by police, churches, etc., possible

SITE SUPERVISOR

Supervision of defendants in community service sentencing projects

Handyman skills and motivational abilities helpful

Good entry-level position

SUPPORT SERVICES COORDINATOR

Assistance to nonviolent misdemeanants in alternative sentencing programs with social service needs

Knowledge of social service programs required

Experience in counseling required

VICTIM SERVICES PERSONNEL

Assistance to crime victims

Exposure to disturbing crisis situations

Ability to work well under pressure

Exercise

Of the above-listed careers, which position most interests you?

_____

_____

_____

_____

_____

_____

_____

Careers in Forensic Science/Criminalistics

Here are some career options if you are interested in the area of forensics/criminalistics.

ARSON SPECIALIST

Employment by various police and fire departments and insurance
    companies

Determination of origin and cause of fire through collection of
    evidence

BALLISTICS SPECIALIST

Examination of weapons used in commission of crimes

Identification of guns

CRIME SCENE INVESTIGATOR

Collection of evidence at crime scenes

Preservation of evidence for processing

Testimony in court proceedings possible

DOCUMENT SPECIALIST

Comparison of questioned handwriting with known handwriting

Determination of handwriting as legal or forged

FINGERPRINT SPECIALIST

Responsibility for collecting, classifying, analyzing, and identifying fingerprint impressions

Civil service examination required

POLYGRAPH SPECIALIST

Examination of individuals to discern truthful and false responses

Special skills and training required

SEROLOGY SPECIALIST

Laboratory analyses of body fluids (such as blood, urine, semen)

Performance of extensive chemical tests to determine level of drugs or alcohol

TOOL MARK SPECIALIST

Identification of tools or objects used by criminals at scene of crimes

Investigation of motor vehicle thefts

Exercise

Of the above-listed careers, which position most interests you?

_____

_____

_____

_____

_____

_____

Careers in Corrections

The following list presents job opportunities in corrections.

ACADEMIC TEACHER

Employment at all levels within correctional facility

Instruction offered in basic remedial courses designed to increase inmates' rudimentary English, reading, and/or math abilities

Time focused on grading papers, preparing lesson plans, and attending meetings

CASEWORK/HIV SPECIALIST

Help for HIV-infected inmates in coping with their emotional and health-related concerns

Genuine concern/care for others

Bachelor's degree required

CLASSIFICATION AND TREATMENT DIRECTOR

Application of principles of management to overall planning of correctional programs

Assignment of inmates to particular programs as well as review of inmate case reports

Ability to work well with others

CLINICAL PSYCHOLOGIST

Work focused on inmates

Member of interdisciplinary health care team

Doctorate required

CORRECTIONAL TREATMENT SPECIALIST

Provision of guidance/support to inmate population

Work focused solely on inmate population

Assistance to others in determining inmates' special needs

CORRECTIONS COUNSELOR

Guidance and counsel for inmates during their incarceration

Provision of individual and group counseling sessions

Strong interest in helping others

CORRECTIONS OFFICER

Care, custody, and control of inmates

Observation and supervision of inmates in correctional facility

Rotating shifts

Excellent interpersonal communication skills

DETENTION DEPUTY

Supervision and control of detainees in jails

Enforcement of security rules within institutions

Provision of services and information to detainees

High school diploma or GED

U.S. citizenship required

Minimum age limit of 21

EDUCATION COUNSELOR

Provision of counseling services to inmates

Assistance to ensure that inmates' choice of programs are relevant
to their goals

Evaluation of inmates' progress

JUVENILE JUSTICE COUNSELOR

Counsel to juveniles assigned to state youth divisions

Work with varied types of juveniles (from those in need of supervision to hard-core adolescents)

Work frequently performed in institutional settings

JUVENILE PROBATION OFFICER

Intake, investigation, and supervision services to family court for juveniles

Desire to work with youth and their families required

Ability to manage heavy caseload

PAROLE OFFICER

Employment in correctional facility or private agency

Investigation of and action on parole violations

Training in use of firearms required

PRERELEASE PROGRAM, CORRECTIONS COUNSELOR

Provision of counsel for clients

Help for clients in their transition from custody to society

Ability to interact well with inmates

PRERELEASE PROGRAM, EMPLOYMENT COUNSELOR

Provision of vocational guidance for those soon to be released from incarceration

Strong communication skills required

Placement of hard-to-employ clients

PRERELEASE PROGRAM, HALFWAY HOUSE MANAGER

Position similar to that of corrections officer/prison administrator

Strong administrative skills required

Willingness to work during any shift and on weekends

PROBATION OFFICER

Presentence reports and evaluations concerning release conditions

Work focused on rehabilitation of offenders as well as their supervision upon their release

Human relations skills required

RECREATION COUNSELOR

Arrangement and supervision of inmates' social activities

Ability to organize and motivate participants

Promotion of emotional, physical, and social well-being of inmates

SUBSTANCE ABUSE SPECIALIST

Employment in correctional institutions as well as prerelease and other alternative detention programs

Provision of individual and group counseling

Specific training in substance abuse possibly required

VOCATIONAL COUNSELOR

Provision of educational programs in vocational specialties

Determination of inmates' learning needs and abilities as well as other information

Provision of other career training through work programs

WARDEN

Overall supervision and administration of correctional facility
Plans for, direction of, and coordination of programs
Knowledge of all phases of corrections operations

Exercise

Of the above-listed careers, which position most interests you?

_____

_____

_____

_____

_____

_____

_____

_____

_____

_____

_____

_____

Careers in Private Security

The criminal justice careers identified in this section would allow you to work in the private sector.

ADMINISTRATOR/MANAGER

Leadership position entailing ability to make policy decisions

Responsibility for personnel administration

INVESTIGATOR

Ability to work well with people and collect evidence

Ability to work well under pressure

PROTECTIVE SPECIALIST/SECURITY OFFICER

Patrol of designated areas

Duties of checking gates, locks, windows, and doors

Training in firearms and self-defense preferred

TECHNICIAN

Working knowledge of operation of technological equipment required

Exercise

Of the above-listed careers, which position most interests you?

_____

_____

_____

_____

Career in Criminology

The following section focuses on the position of criminologist.

DEFINITION

Criminologists are academics who study crime, criminology, and the law. They provide theoretical explanations of delinquent and criminal behaviors, analyze criminal law, and study criminal patterns.

They are primarily involved in teaching, researching, and publishing. They may study drug addiction, juvenile justice and delinquency, policing and police policy, corrections, correctional administration and policy, normal human behavior and criminal behavior, forensics, and victimology.

Criminologists analyze psychological, sociological, and biological factors related to criminals.

They may be involved in community initiatives as well as evaluations and policy projects with local and state criminal justice agencies.

EDUCATION AND TRAINING

At minimum, criminologists need to complete a master's degree program in criminal justice or criminology; those working in universities may have a Ph.D. Programs in criminology generally cover criminal behavior as found in sociology, psychology, and criminal justice.

SALARY

Criminologists teaching at universities earn between $32,270 and $76,000.

By 2001, average U.S. salaries for professors were $76,000; associate professors, $55,300; and assistant professors, $34,700.

Salary for instructors averages $34,700; for lecturers, it is approximately $38,000.

Faculty in four-year institutions earn a higher average salary than those in two-year schools.

WORKPLACE

Criminologists may work in universities teaching criminology, legal studies, and law while conducting their own research. State and federal criminal justice agencies employ criminologists as researchers and policy advisors. Others are in private practice, providing consultation on such issues as law reform, juvenile justice, crime statistics, and adult corrections. They may write and publish books.

Exercise

Does a career as a criminologist interest you? If so, why?

_____

_____

_____

_____

_____

CHAPTER SEVEN

HOT JOBS IN CRIMINAL JUSTICE

In the following sections, we provide many exciting jobs that are available in criminal justice–related fields. See which ones appeal to you.

Administrative Office of the U.S. Courts

These jobs are associated with the court system.

- U.S. probation officer
- Pretrial services officer
- Statistician
- Investigator

REQUIREMENTS

Bachelor's degree from accredited college or university (to qualify applicant for position of probation officer at GS-5 level)

Minimum of two years of general work experience

Bachelor's degree in accepted field of study, including criminology, criminal justice, penology, correctional administration, social work, sociology, public administration, or psychology (to qualify applicant for immediate employment at GS-5 level)

One year of graduate study (to qualify applicant for employment at GS-7 level)

Master's degree (to qualify applicant for advanced placement)

Maximum age of 37

Excellent physical health

SALARY

GS-5 or GS-7 salary level (depending on education and work history)

Direct inquiries to:

> Administrative Office of the U.S. Courts
> Personnel Office
> Washington, D.C. 20544
>
> Phone: (202) 273-1297
> Website: http://www.uscourts.gov

Federal Air Marshal (FAM)

The media has publicized the job of federal air marshal since the terrorist attacks of September 11, 2001.

REQUIREMENTS

Maximum age of 40

U.S. citizenship

Eligibility for top secret security clearance

One year of professional investigative/law enforcement experience or bachelor's degree

Completion of criminal investigator's course at Federal Law Enforcement Training Center (after appointment)

SALARY

Salary range of $35,000–$80,000 (depending on applicant qualifications)

Direct inquiries to:

U.S. Department of Homeland Security
Washington, D.C.

Phone: (202) 282-8000
Websites: http://www.dhs.gov
http://www.jobsearch.usa.jobs.cpm.gov

Bureau of Alcohol, Tobacco, and Firearms (BATF)

Many job possibilities exist with the Bureau of Alcohol, Tobacco, and Firearms:

- Special agent
- Explosives expert
- Firearms specialist
- Bomb scene investigator
- Liquor law violations investigator
- Fingerprint identification specialist
- Intelligence specialist
- Forensic chemist

REQUIREMENTS

Completion of Treasury Enforcement Agent Examination, field interview, and thorough background investigation

U.S. citizenship

Age between 21 and 35

Good physical health

Eyesight no less than 20/100 uncorrected (and at least 20/30 corrected in one eye and 20/20 in the other)

Eight weeks of specialized training at Federal Law Enforcement Training Center in Glynco, Georgia (new agents)

GS-5 salary level (bachelor's degree) or GS-7 salary level (depending on geographic area of assignment, possible salary increase from 16 percent to 30 percent above base level)

Direct inquiries to:

Bureau of Alcohol, Tobacco, and Firearms, U.S. Treasury Dept.
650 Massachusetts Avenue N.W., Room 4100
Washington, D.C. 20226

Phone: (202) 927-8423
Website: http://atf.treas.gov

Corrections Officer

If you are interested in working directly with inmate populations, consider a job in corrections. Potential jobs are:

- Detention deputy (county)
- Corrections officer (county, state, federal)
- Jailer

REQUIREMENTS

High school diploma or GED

Valid driver's license

U.S. citizenship

Minimum age of 21 (for some jurisdictions, minimum set at age 19)

Successful completion of written and physical entry-level examinations

Successful completion of background check

Basic corrections officer training program (after appointment)

SALARY

Entry-level annual salary range of $26,000–$40,000

Direct inquiries to county, state, or federal corrections agency in geographic area of interest.

Crime Scene Investigator

Solving crimes by examining locations and evidence is the focus of these careers. Potential jobs are:

- Crime scene technician
- Investigator
- Evidence custodian

REQUIREMENTS

High school diploma (college degree preferred by some agencies)

Crime scene technology course work

Valid driver's license

Successful completion of background investigation

Law enforcement experience possibly required for position of crime scene investigator (other agencies hire civilian crime scene investigators)

SALARY

Entry-level salary range of $30,000–$40,000 (depending on agency and geographic location)

Direct inquiries to local, county, or state law enforcement agency in geographic area of interest.

Department of Homeland Security (DHS)

Homeland security is one of the newest fields in criminal justice, but many of the positions (e.g., Secret Service, Border Patrol, Immigration and Naturalization) have been around for decades. Experts in domestic and international terrorism, communications, emergency planning, and immigration are just the tip of the iceberg. As you can see, professionals in homeland security work in many different areas.

If you have a keen mind and want to make a real difference in the world and in the safety of your country, homeland security might be the job for you. Several examples of homeland security positions are:

- Homeland security specialist
- Emergency management
- Communications specialist
- Terrorism expert
- Airport security screener

Due to the consolidation of a number of federal criminal justice agencies into DHS, we would encourage you to further research specific positions and qualifications at the DHS website listed below.

Direct inquiries to:

U.S. Department of Homeland Security
Washington, D.C.

Phone: (202) 282-8000
Websites: http://www.dhs.gov and
http://www.jobsearch.usa.jobs.cpm.gov

Dispatcher

If the area of communications appeals to you, consider a job in dispatching. Potentianl jobs include:

- Telecommunications specialist (dispatcher)
- Call taker

REQUIREMENTS

High school diploma
Excellent typing skills

Sound judgment

Successful completion of entry-level testing

Successful completion of telecommunications training program

Ability to multitask

Excellent interpersonal communications skills

SALARY

Varied entry-level salaries (average salary range of
$25,000–$35,000)

Direct inquiries to local, county, state, or federal agency in geographic area of interest.

Drug Enforcement Administration (DEA)

The Drug Enforcement Administration offers several excellent
career choices. Potential job opportunities include:

- Special agent
- Criminal investigator
- Chemist
- Intelligence research specialist

REQUIREMENTS

U.S. citizenship

Age between 21 and 36

Good health

Successful completion of comprehensive background investigation

Valid driver's license

Excellent oral and written communications skills

Three years of job-related experience

Overall college GPA of 2.9

GPA of 3.5 in major field of study

Standing in upper one-third of graduating class

Membership in scholastic national honor society

One year of successful graduate study or one year of specialized experience (defined as "progressively responsible investigative experience")

Willingness to travel frequently

Submission to urinalysis test designed to detect presence of controlled substances

Successful completion of two-month training at FBI training center in Quantico, Virginia

Special agents: Excellent physical condition, sharp hearing, and uncorrected vision of at least 20/200 (corrected vision of 20/20 in one eye and at least 20/40 in the other)

SALARY

GS-7 salary level for entry-level positions for individuals with four-year college degree (higher pay grades for individuals possessing additional education and experience)

Direct inquiries to:

Drug Enforcement Administration
Office of Personnel, Recruitment, and Placement
400 6th Street, N.W., Room 2558
Washington, D.C. 20024

Phone: (800) 332-4288
Website: http://www.usdoj.gov/dea

Federal Bureau of Investigation (FBI)

Perhaps one of the most recognized positions in criminal justice is an FBI special agent, but many other job opportunities present themselves.

- Special agent
- Crime laboratory technician
- Ballistics technician
- Computer operator
- Fingerprint specialist
- Explosives examiner
- Document expert
- Other nonagent technical positions

REQUIREMENTS

Age between 23 and 37

Excellent physical health

Uncorrected vision of not less than 20/200 (corrected to 20/20 in one eye and 20/40 in the other)

Good hearing

U.S. citizenship

Valid driver's license

Successful completion of background investigation check

Bachelor's degree or law degree from accredited college or university

Successful completion of initial written examination

Intensive formal interview

Submission to urinalysis

Polygraph possibly required

Programs exist in the areas of law, accounting, languages, and engineering/science as well as a general diversified area, which requires a minimum of three years of full-time work experience, preferably with a law enforcement agency. The FBI emphasizes education and favors degrees in law, graduate studies, business, and accounting. Most nonagent technical career paths also require a bachelor's degree or an advanced degree and U.S. citizenship.

SALARY

Special agents: GS-10 grade at entry

Field assignments: GS-13 grade

Supervisory and management positions: GS-13 grade

High-cost-of-living supplement (ranging from 4 percent to 16 percent) paid in specified geographic areas

Direct inquiries to:

Federal Bureau of Investigation
U.S. Department of Justice
9th Street and Pennsylvania Avenue, N.W.
Washington, D.C. 20535

Phone: (202) 324-4991 (or check your local phone book)
Website: http://www.fbi.gov

Federal Bureau of Prisons (FBP)

If you would like to work directly with inmates, consider one of the following careers.

- Corrections officer
- Psychologist
- Physician
- Nurse
- Chaplain
- Corrections/drug treatment specialist
- Safety specialist
- Teacher
- Program officer
- Vocational instructor

REQUIREMENTS

U.S. citizenship

Maximum age of 37

Successful completion of employee interview

Successful completion of physical examination

Successful completion of background investigation

Bachelor's degree (corrections officer)

Successful completion of in-service training at Federal Law
Enforcement Training Academy at Glynco, Georgia

SALARY

Corrections officers: GS-5 at entry (six months or more of graduate
education in criminal justice or any social science for possible
GS-6 or higher, and possible advancement to higher level after
six months of satisfactory service).

Direct inquiries to:

Federal Bureau of Prisons
320 First Street, N.W., Room 460
Washington, D.C. 20524

Phone: (202) 307-3175
Website: http://bop.gov

Immigration and Customs Enforcement (ICE)

Difficulties along our country's borders, such as smuggling and illegal immigrants, are some of the issues these job holders would be dealing with. Positions include:

- Criminal investigator
- Special agent
- Customs inspector
- Canine enforcement officer

- Import specialist
- Intelligence research specialist
- Computer operator
- Auditor
- Customs aide
- Investigative assistant/clerk

REQUIREMENTS

U.S. citizenship

Maximum age of 34

Successful completion of physical exam

Successful completion of personal background investigation

Submission to urinalysis for controlled substances

Relevant work experience required

REQUIREMENTS FOR HIGHER-LEVEL PAY GRADE

One year of specialized experience (e.g., "responsible criminal investigator" or comparable experience)

Bachelor's degree with demonstration of superior academic achievement (3.0 GPA in all courses completed at time of application, or 3.5 GPA in applicant's major field of study, or rank in upper one-third of graduating class), or membership in scholastic national honor society

One year of successful graduate study in related field

OTHER REQUIREMENTS

Willingness to travel frequently

Ability to work overtime

Capability to work under stressful conditions

Willingness to carry weapons and ability to qualify regularly with firearms

SALARY

GS-5 or GS-7 salary level at entry (depending on education and prior work experience)

Direct inquiries to:

Office of Human Resources
U.S. Customs Service
1301 Constitution Avenue, N.W., Room 220
Washington, D.C. 20229

Phone: (202) 634-2534
Website: http://www.customs.treas.gov

Immigration and Naturalization Service (INS) Border Patrol

As with the careers provided above, these jobs target problems along the U.S. borders. Jobs include:

- Special agent
- Border Patrol agent
- Immigration inspector
- Deportation officer

REQUIREMENTS

U.S. citizenship

Age 21–34

Bachelor's degree or three years of related work experience

Excellent physical condition, with good eyesight and hearing

Submission to urinalysis screening

Emotional and mental stability

No felony conviction or record of improper or criminal conduct

Border Patrol agents: Proficiency in Spanish and/or French (Canadian Border)

SALARY

GS-5 salary level (with bachelor's degree)

Possible GS-7 salary level (with exceptional experience or education)

Direct inquiries to:

Immigration and Naturalization Service
U.S. Department of Justice
4251 1 Street, N.W., Room 220
Washington, D.C. 20536

Phone: (800) 238-1945
Website: http://www.ins.usdoj.gov

Municipal or County Police Officer

If you are attracted to law enforcement in a specific area, consider these career choices.

- Police officer/deputy sheriff
- Detective/investigator
- Crime scene specialist
- SWAT member

REQUIREMENTS

High school diploma or GED (college degree preferred or required by some agencies)

U.S. citizenship

Minimum age of 21

Valid driver's license

Good moral character/successful completion of background check

Successful completion of written and physical entrance exams

Successful completion of Police Academy after appointment

Varied entry-level salaries (department to department as well as regionally throughout the United States), with range of $30,000 – $40,000

Direct inquiries to local city police department or county sheriff's office in geographic area of interest.

State Police Officer

Law enforcement personnel are needed not only at the municipal and county levels but at the state level. Potential jobs include:

- Trooper
- Detective/special agent
- Crime scene investigator
- Forensic lab specialist
- Hazardous materials specialist
- SWAT member

REQUIREMENTS

Minimum age of 21

U.S. citizenship

High school diploma (some agencies prefer or require college degree)

Successful completion of written and physical exams

Good moral character/successful completion of background check

Successful completion of basic training (after appointment)

Direct inquiries to state police or highway patrol in geographic area of interest.

U.S. Marshal Service

For a law enforcement position that transcends local and state boundaries, try a career with the U.S. Marshal Service.

- Court security
- Fugitive investigations
- Personal and witness security
- Asset seizure
- Special operations
- Transportation and custody of federal prisoners

REQUIREMENTS

Successful completion of comprehensive written exam

Successful completion of complete background investigation

Oral interview

Excellent physical condition

Bachelor's degree or three years of "responsible experience"

U.S. citizenship

Age between 21 and 36

Valid driver's license

SALARY

GS-5 or GS-7 salary level (depending on education)

Direct inquiries to:

U.S. Marshal Service
600 Army-Navy Drive
Arlington, VA 22202

Phone: (202) 307-9600
Website: http://www.usdoj.gov/marshals

U.S. Secret Service

Last but by no means least would be a career in the U.S. Secret Service. Careers include:

- Special agent
- Uniformed division police officer
- Special officer

REQUIREMENTS

Successful completion of Treasury Enforcement Agent examination

Bachelor's degree from accredited college or university with superior academic achievement or one year of graduate study in related field (e.g., criminology, law enforcement, police science, police administration, business administration, accounting)

Excellent physical condition (including at least 20/40 vision in each eye, correctable to 20/20)

Successful completion of thorough background investigation

Valid driver's license

Submission to urinalysis test for illegal drugs

Ability to qualify for top secret security clearance

SALARY

Special agents: GS-5 or GS-7 (depending on education)

High-cost-of-living supplement (ranging from 4 percent to 16 percent) in specified geographic areas

Applicants are not accepted earlier than nine months prior to graduation.

Direct inquiries to:

U.S. Secret Service
1800 G Street, N.W., Room 912
Washington, D.C. 20223

Phone: (888) 813-8777
Website: http://www.treas.gov/usss

CHAPTER EIGHT

WHO TO CONTACT?

Criminal Justice Standards and Training Agencies

Every state in the United States has authority to establish requirements for becoming a criminal justice professional in their respective state. State requirements vary from state to state. Therefore, if you are serious about a criminal justice career, you will need to contact either the local agency you intend to apply to or the state's criminal justice standards and training agency that establishes training and entry-level requirements for that state and jurisdiction.

To assist you in determining each state's employment and training criteria, we have provided contact information for each state as well as the District of Columbia's training and standards board. Also, keep in mind that each individual criminal justice agency may have additional requirements that a candidate must meet in order to be hired. You should contact those individual agencies (e.g., Chicago Police Department, Florida Highway Patrol, FBI) to determine their specific hiring criteria.

Law Enforcement Standards and Training: State Agencies

Each state (and Washington, D.C.) has at least one state agency you can contact for more career information.

Alabama

Alabama Police Officers Standards and Training
P.O. Box 300075
Montgomery, Alabama 36130-0075

(334) 242-4045   Fax: (334) 242-4633

Alaska

Alaska Police Standards
4500 Diplomacy Drive
Anchorage, Alaska 99508

(907) 269-7408   Fax: (907) 269-7333

Arizona

Arizona Peace Officer Standards and Training
2543 East University Drive
Phoenix, Arizona 85034

(602) 223-2514 ext. 238   Fax: (602) 244-0477

Arkansas

Arkansas Law Enforcement Training Academy
P.O. Box 3106
East Camden, Arkansas 71701

(870) 574-1810   Fax: (870) 574-2706

California

California Commission of Police Officer Standards and Training
1601 Alahambra Boulevard
Sacramento, California 95816-7053

(916) 227-2803   Fax: (916) 227-2801

Colorado

Colorado Police Officers Standards and Training
1525 Sherman Avenue, 5th Floor
Denver, Colorado 80203

(303) 866-5692   Fax: (303) 866-4139

Connecticut

Police Standards and Training
285 Preston Avenue
Meriden, Connecticut 06450-4891

(203) 238-6505   Fax: (203) 238-6643

Delaware

Delaware State Police Training
1453 North DuPont Highway
Dover, Delaware 19901

(302) 739-5903   Fax: (302) 739-5945

District of Columbia

District of Columbia Police Training and Standards Board
300 Indiana Avenue, N.W., Suite 5031
Washington, D.C. 20001

(202) 727-1516   Fax: (202) 727-5101

Florida

Florida Department of Law Enforcement
P.O. Box 1489
Tallahassee, Florida 32302-1489

(850) 410-8600   Fax: (850) 410-8606

Georgia

Executive Director
Federal Law Enforcement Accreditation
RRD TH 375
Glynco, Georgia

(912) 267-2586

Georgia Peace Officers Standards and Training Council
5000 Austell-Power Springs Road, Suite 261
Austell, Georgia 30106

(770) 732-5974   Fax: (770) 732-5952

Hawaii

Honolulu Police Department
801 South Beretania Street
Honolulu, Hawaii 96813

(808) 529-3175   Fax: (808) 529-3030

Idaho

Idaho Peace Officer Standards and Training
P.O. Box 700
Meridian, Idaho 83680-0700

(208) 884-7250   Fax: (208) 884-7295

Illinois

Illinois Law Enforcement Training and Standards Board
600 S. Second Street, Suite 300
Springfield, Illinois 62704-2542

(217) 785-5910   Fax: (217) 524-5350

Indiana

Indiana Law Enforcement Academy
5402 Sugar Grove, P.O. Box 313
Plainfield, Indiana 46168

(317) 839-5191   Fax: (317) 839-9741

Iowa

Iowa Law Enforcement Academy
P.O. Box 130
Johnston, Iowa 50131-0130

(515) 242-5357   Fax: (515) 242-5471

Kansas

Kansas Law Enforcement Training Center
P.O. Box 647
Hutchinson, Kansas 67504-0647

(620) 694-1400   Fax: (620) 694-1420

Kentucky

Kentucky Department of Criminal Justice Training
521 Lancaster Road, Funderburk Building
Richmond, Kentucky 40475-3137

(859) 622-2217　　Fax: (859) 622-3162

Louisiana

Louisiana Police Officers Standards and Training Council
1885 Wooddale Boulevard, Room 208
Baton Rouge, Louisiana 20806

(225) 925-4942　　Fax: (225) 925-1998

Maine

Criminal Justice Academy
15 Oak Grove Road
Vassalboro, Maine 04989

(207) 877-8008　　Fax: (207) 877-8027

Maryland

Maryland Police & Correctional Training
6852 4th Street
Sykesville, Maryland 21784

(410) 875-3400　　Fax: (410) 875-3500

Massachusetts

Massachusetts Criminal Justice Training Council
484 Shea Memorial Drive
South Weymouth, Massachusetts 02190

(617) 727-7827　　Fax: (781) 331-5187

Michigan

Commission on Law Enforcement Standards
7426 North Canal Road
Lansing, Michigan 48913

(517) 322-1417　　Fax: (517) 322-6439

Minnesota

Board of Peace Officer Standards and Training
1600 University Avenue, Suite 200
St. Paul, Minnesota 55104-3825

(651) 643-3063   Fax: (651) 643-3072

Mississippi

Board of Law Enforcement Standards and Training
37501-55 Frontage Road, North
Jackson, Mississippi 39211

(601) 987-3050   Fax: (601) 987-3086

Missouri

Missouri Peace Officer Standards and Training
P.O. Box 749
Jefferson City, Missouri 65102-0749

(573) 526-2765   Fax: (573) 751-5399

Montana

Montana Police Officers Standards and Training
P.O. Box 201408
Helena, Montana 59620-1408

(406) 444-3605   Fax: (406) 444-4722

Nebraska

Nebraska Law Enforcement Training Center
3600 North Academy Road
Grand Island, Nebraska 68801-0403

(308) 385-6030 ext.311   Fax: (308) 385-6032

Nevada

Commission on Peace Officers Standards and Training
5587 Wa Pai Shone Avenue
Carson City, Nevada 89701

(775) 647-7678 ext. 223   Fax: (775) 687-4911

New Hampshire

Police Standards and Training
17 Institute Drive
Concord, New Hampshire 03301-7413
(603) 271-2133   Fax: (603) 271-1785

New Jersey

New Jersey Division of Criminal Justice Police Training Commission
25 Market Street
P.O. Box 085
Trenton, New Jersey 08625-0085
(609) 984-0960   Fax: (609) 984-4473

New Mexico

Department of Public Safety Training and Recruiting Division
4491 Cerrillos Road
Santa Fe, New Mexico 87507-9721
(505) 827-9265   Fax: (505) 827-3449

New York

New York Division of Criminal Justice Services
4 Tower Place
Albany, New York 12203-3764
(518) 457-6101   Fax: (518) 457-3089

North Carolina

North Carolina Criminal Justice Education and Training
P.O. Box 149
Raleigh, North Carolina 27602
(919) 716-6470   Fax: (919) 716-6752

North Dakota

North Dakota Police Officers Standards and Training Board
P.O. Box 1054
Bismarck, North Dakota 58502-1054
(701) 328-5500   Fax: (701) 328-5510

Ohio

Ohio Peace Officer Training Academy
P.O. Box 309
London, Ohio 43140
(614) 466-2771   Fax: (614) 728-5150

Oklahoma

Oklahoma Council on Law Enforcement Education and Training
P.O. Box 11476
Oklahoma City, Oklahoma 73136-0476
(405) 425-2751   Fax: (405) 425-2773

Oregon

Department of Public Safety Standards and Training
550 North Monmouth Avenue
Monmouth, Oregon 97361
(503) 378-2100 ext. 2201   Fax: (503) 378-3330

Pennsylvania

Pennsylvania Municipal Police Officers Education and Training
    Commission
8002 Bretz Drive
Harrisburg, Pennsylvania 17112-9748
(717) 346-7749   Fax: (717) 346-7782

Rhode Island

Police Academy
Flanagan Campus
1762 Louisquisset Pike
Lincoln, Rhode Island 02865
(401) 722-58081   Fax: (401) 722-3151

South Carolina

South Carolina Criminal Justice Academy
P.O. Box 1993
Blythewood, South Carolina 29206-1993
(803) 896-7779   Fax: (803) 896-8347

South Dakota

Rol Kebach Criminal Justice Training Center
East Highway 34, 500 East Capitol
Pierre, South Dakota 57501-7070
(605) 773-3584   Fax: (605) 773-7203

Tennessee

Tennessee Law Enforcement Training Academy
3025 Lebanon Road
Nashville, Tennessee 37214-2217
(615) 741-4448   Fax: (615) 741-3366

Texas

Texas Commission on Law Enforcement Officer Standards and
    Training
6330 U.S. WY 290 East, Suite 200
Austin, Texas 787723
(512) 936-7700   Fax: (512) 936-7714

Utah

Peace Officer Standards and Training
P.O. Box 141775
Salt Lake City, Utah 84114-1775
(801) 965-4370   Fax: (801) 965-4619

Vermont

Vermont Criminal Justice Training Council
317 Sanatorium Road
Pittsford, Vermont 05763
(802) 483-6228 ext. 20   Fax: (802) 482-2343

Virginia

Standards and Training, Department of Criminal Justice Services
805 East Broad Street
Richmond, Virginia 23219
(804) 786-8001   Fax: (804) 786-0410

Washington

Washington State Criminal Justice Training Commission
19010 1st Avenue, South
Burien, Washington 98148
(206) 835-7347   Fax: (206) 439-3893

West Virginia

Criminal Justice and Highway Safety
1204 Kanawha Boulevard East
Charleston, West Virginia 25301
(304) 558-8814   Fax: (304) 558-0391

Wisconsin

Wisconsin Training and Standards Bureau
P.O. Box 7070
Madison, Wisconsin 53707-7070
(608) 266-7864   Fax: (608) 266-7869

Wyoming

Wyoming Peace Officers Standards and Training
1710 Pacific Avenue
Cheyenne, Wyoming 82002
(307) 777-6619   Fax: (307) 638-9706

Federal Agencies

Here we provide you with an alphabetized listing of many federal agencies and their contact information.

Bureau of Alcohol, Tobacco, and Firearms (ATF)

Office of Public and Governmental Affairs
650 Massachusetts Avenue, N.W., Room 8290
Washington, D.C. 20226

www.persdiv@atf.gov

www.agentinfo@atf.gov

Drug Enforcement Administration (DEA)

Special Agent Recruitment
Drug Enforcement Administration
700 Army Navy Drive
Arlington, Virginia 22202

(800) DEA-4288

www.dea.gov

Federal Bureau of Investigation (FBI)

935 Pennsylvania Avenue, N.W.
Washington, D.C. 20535
(202) 324-3000

www.fbi.gov

Immigration and Customs Enforcement (ICE)

U.S. Department of Homeland Security
425 I Street
Washington, D.C., 20536

(202) 514-2895

www.dhs.gov www.jobsearch.usa.jobs.opm.gov

Secret Service

Personnel Division
1800 G Street, N.W., Room 912
Washington, D.C. 20223

(202) 406-05800 or (888) 813-8777

www.secretservice.gov

U.S. Customs and Border Protection

1300 Pennsylvania Avenue, N.W.
Washington, D.C. 20229

(202) 354-1000

www.dhs.gov

www.jobsearch.usa.jobs.opm.gov U.S.